THE GOSPEL MADE SIMPLE

The Gospel Made Simple | Copyright © 2019 by Cherie Anderson

All rights reserved solely by the author. The author guarantees all contents are original and do not infringe upon the legal rights of any other person or work. No part of this book may be reproduced in any form without the permission of the author.

Scripture quotations are from the ESV® Bible (The Holy Bible, English Standard Version®), copyright © 2001 by Crossway, a publishing ministry of Good News Publishers. Used by permission. All rights reserved. Represented by Tyndale House Publishers, Inc. Scripture quotations marked (NLT) are taken from the Holy Bible, New Living Translation, copyright ©1996, 2004, 2015 by Tyndale House Foundation. Used by permission of Tyndale House Publishers, Inc., Carol Stream, Illinois 60188. All rights reserved. Scripture quotations marked (NIV) are taken from the Holy Bible, New International Version®, NIV®. Copyright © 1973, 1978, 1984, 2011 by Biblica, Inc.™ Used by permission of Zondervan. All rights reserved worldwide. www.zondervan.com The "NIV" and "New International Version" are trademarks registered in the United States Patent and Trademark Office by Biblica, Inc.™ Scripture quotations marked (AMP) are taken from the Amplified Bible, Copyright © 1954, 1958, 1962, 1964, 1965, 1987 by The Lockman Foundation. Used by permission. Scripture quotations from The Authorized (King James) Version. Rights in the Authorized Version in the United Kingdom are vested in the Crown. Reproduced by permission of the Crown's patentee, Cambridge University Press Scripture quotations taken from the New American Standard Bible® (NASB), Copyright © 1960, 1962, 1963, 1968, 1971, 1972, 1973, 1975, 1977, 1995 by The Lockman Foundation Used by permission. www.Lockman.org

*Scriptures marked PARA are passages from the Holy Bible that have been paraphrased by the author.

ISBN-13: 9781687366467

Tall Pine Books: An Imprint of Pulpit to Page
|| tallpinebooks.com

THE GOSPEL MADE SIMPLE

CHERIE ANDERSON

TALL PINE

CONTENTS

Foreword	vii
Preface	ix
1. My Testimony	1
2. The Time is Now	11
3. Become Unstoppable	17
4. Happiness vs. Righteousness Gospel	31
5. The Law's Purpose	37
6. Witnessing to the Good Person	45
7. Treasure Hunting	51
8. Witnessing to Family and Friends	59
9. Allow God Out of the Sunday Morning Box	69
10. Build a Bridge	83
11. Oh no, you didn't, Oh yes, I did!	93
12. Overcoming the Top 10 Objections	103
13. Conclusion	123
Resources	126
Sources	128

Within the pages of this book, Cherie has given us tools to make what so many feel is difficult, "Made easy." This book is a must to motivate everyone who longs to share their hope in Jesus Christ but feel inadequate. You won't be disappointed!!

—STEVE VAGGALIS, Pastor of *Destiny Worship Center*
Destin, Florida

Cherie Anderson's book, *The Gospel Made Simple*, is an inspiring and encouraging challenge to every believer to share our faith. Her practical and scripture-filled approach will help make evangelism easy in our daily lives and prepares us to become great harvesters of souls in the coming great revival in the earth. This book is timely!

—JANE HAMON, Co-Apostle of *Vision Church @ Christian International* | Author of, *Dreams and Visions*, *The Deborah Company*, *The Cyrus Decree*, *Discernment*

FOREWORD

As an author of two books on evangelism, one of which was used as a textbook at Rhema bible college. Cherie's book is well-written and needed in such a time as this. Your encouragement to get out of the church walls and share your faith was in deed inspiring. Her use of the Scriptures drove home much needed points that are often ignored in modern day American Christianity. She balances hard-hitting with soft touches to encourage each one of us to fulfill the Great Commission.

The *happiness gospel* chapter was almost prophetic and every believer should seriously look at their own heart "to see if we are in the faith." Her chapter on Islam gives many good pointers to encourage God's people to share their faith with this aggressive religion. She balances grace and repentance, the need for sharing your faith without guilt demonstrates she has the skilled tongue of a doctor bringing a baby into the world. I especially enjoyed the section on apologetics as we tend to avoid confrontation. Her chapter on overcoming fear was especially encouraging. She also has a chapter on combining the gifts of the Spirit and evangelism. Her teaching on Treasure Hunting is adventurous to say the least. I also appreciate the action steps at the end of each chapter. This anointed book covers so many topics and it is a must read for every believer. I have known Cherie for nearly 20 years and she lives what she preaches.

—TOM STAMMAN, President of *Impact Ministries International*

PREFACE

It is my deepest hope that this book will not only inspire but *equip* you so you can feel more confident about sharing the gospel of Jesus Christ. It is also my desire to dispel some misconceptions and expose the devil's lies and devices that keep way too many Christians silent.

If you have been silent, I challenge you to be silent no longer. No matter your age or background—you have a destiny and you were created to take part in building the kingdom of God and fulfilling the Great Commission. Don't just be a spectator sitting on the sidelines , but be the one who is in the game, fulfilling the call of God on your life and making a difference in the life of another.

Doing amazing things for God doesn't mean you have to stand on a platform or go on a mission trip. It's being a witness for Jesus Christ in the trenches of the day to day. Make it happen by taking those steps of faith into the unknown and see how Father God will meet you there and take you the distance. Let's not live life with regrets and what if's.

It is urgent that we take action now and speak the truth in love because we carry the answer people are searching for, Jesus Christ the hope of glory! He is the cure for the cancer that is ravaging their soul and you can be the instrument that can save their life!

Romans 10:13-15 (NLT) For "Everyone who calls on the name of the LORD will be saved."But how can they call on him to save them unless they believe in him? And how can they believe in him if they have never heard about him? And how can they hear about him unless someone tells them? And how will anyone go and tell them without being sent? That is why the Scriptures say,"How beautiful are the feet of messengers who bring good news!"

—Cherie Anderson

[1]
MY TESTIMONY

I grew up on a farm in South Dakota, the oldest of five children in a Catholic family. We never missed a Sunday and had our designated seats on the front row. I never knew what it was like to not believe in God. But as I grew up, I started to question God's role in my life, I questioned my faith and wondered why many things we did in the name of religion were not in the Bible.

I became a rebellious teenager and young adult. I made a lot of bad decisions that led me down a path I never saw coming. The first was to have an abortion when I was a teenager. Back in the 70's we were led to believe it was just a blob of tissue and that I was way too young to have a child. Our doctor said it would be best if I got an abortion. Little did I know how devastating this one act was to me and my parents. I felt such guilt and shame.

I knew I had disappointed my parents and felt they would never love me again the same. We never spoke of it again which was a mistake to have buried it thinking it would just go away. It only festered and like a cancer it ravaged my mind and spirit. I hung around an older bunch of kids and got into drugs, alcohol and a party lifestyle which led into my 20's. I married when I was 18 and moved to Florida. I thought, yeah, I'm finally free of this small town and thought I was really something. My husband and I continued in the party lifestyle in fact it only got worse.

I would go out with my girlfriends and started living like a single woman. I was leading a double life and had seared my conscious. I wasn't sure what I was looking for or why I was doing these things. I realize now I was in bondage to sin and it had taken me further then I wanted to go and caused me to do things I never thought I would. It was as if I was not in control and I just let my sinful nature run rampant. When I studied the effects of abortion later on, I found this promiscuous and destructive lifestyle was common among women who have abortions.

As my marriage started to crumble and was contemplating divorce, I found out I was pregnant and was not happy about it. I had hit rock bottom! Little did I know this baby was a gift from God and my lifeline! I was reading the paper one day and saw an ad for a Women's

Aglow meeting. Something compelled me to go, so I went all by myself not knowing what to expect. There was a woman there that told of her near-death experience and when there was an altar call to receive forgiveness and accept Jesus as my Savior I went!

Now remember, I grew up Catholic and this was foreign to me. If you wanted to be forgiven of your sins you went to your priest and made confession. I always hated that confession box! I was desperate and wanted escape from myself! The women welcomed me and told me they would meet with me one on one to pray for me. That session was quite intense, they called it *prayers of deliverance.* I had to repent of all I had done and be delivered from my past sins and sever some soul ties to evil things. I felt such a release and freedom from the heaviness of sin. I was invited to a Charismatic non-denominational church and started attending a women's bible study.

I started to learn what it is like to have a personal relationship with Jesus Christ not just a knowledge of God. Through this beautiful group of women, I learned much about myself and grew so much in my faith. We held each other accountable, prayed and cried together. It was critical to my growth at that time. I regularly attended Covenant Community Church and grew in my knowledge of God's Word more than I ever had as a kid because I had never been encouraged to read the Bible for myself.

As I grew in my faith I had recommitted to my marriage and desired to have a Christian home...unfortunately, my husband could not embrace my newfound faith and he refused to change. I had totally given up drugs and alcohol when I learned I was pregnant, but he did not and so the wedge between us grew. Two years after I got saved, we divorced. This really rocked my faith. I had put on the rose-colored glasses and thought *now that I'm a Christian everything is going to be great.*

Little did I know that the devil wanted me back and he was setting me up for a fall. My roots were not deep, and I was very susceptible and naive. The devil is not very creative he uses the same tools repeatedly. In my situation he used a man again. I fell for this guy I thought was my knight in shining armor. I was so infatuated, but our relationship quickly grew into a self-destructive love hate relationship. He was very jealous and then became verbally, and eventually physically, abusive.

Once again I felt like I was losing my true identity, I was a Christian now and this is not what it should look like. I was looking to a man to give me my security and define me. I needed to value who I was as a child of God, and the Lord needed to be the one who gave me my identity, and the control given over to Him! What had happened to my newfound faith? Was it all for nothing, was it real? I started to question everything and how I could become bound, after I had just felt so free. I didn't realize the power that was available within me.

I tell you my story not only so you can know more about me, a flawed individual with a not-too-pretty past, but someone who has a passion to see people live the life Christ died for them to have. Also to remind us of how evil our flesh can be and to offer grace and mercy to others who are struggling in their new found faith. We are saved in an instant, but the sanctification process takes time and our minds have to be renewed. Never forget where you have been so you can remain compassionate and not get judgmental.

I'm not saying we don't hold people accountable for their sin and we shouldn't gloss over sin but we need to offer as much mercy as Christ has offered to us. One of my favorite scriptures is, *those who have been forgiven much, love much* (*see Luke 7*). That is you and me!

THE TURNING POINT

After having gone through divorce and now a bad relationship, my self confidence was shattered. I felt like a failure and worried about how this was all affecting my 3 year old daughter. It wasn't just about *me* but about *her* and wanting better for her. I surrendered myself to the Lord in a way I hadn't before and as I did something rose up in me and I kicked that guy to the curb and recommitted myself to serve Jesus Christ.

My faith in God was still there, I just needed to repent because living in sin had distanced me from God even though I was saved. The devil wanted to bring condemnation on me and keep me down, but God's Word says to us "I forgive you so you too need to forgive yourself and move forward!!" So that is what I did.

I humbled myself, repented, and determined in my heart to live righteously. *James 4:6-10 says God opposes the proud but gives grace to the humble. So humble yourselves before God. Resist the devil, and he will flee from you. Come close to God, and God will come close to you.*

I met my current husband shortly after I left the other guy and he and I determined to love and serve God with all our hearts, and we have for the past 29 years. It hasn't always been easy, but we have been consistently pursuing the knowledge of Jesus Christ and growing in our faith and understanding.

We now have three grown children and two grandchildren. I am an ordained minister, worship leader and I guess now considered an author. My husband and I have gone on many mission trips abroad and witnessed the power of God in miraculous ways. God has done some amazing things in my life and I know there is more to come! As it is for you, as you fully surrender your life to Him.

THE CALL

We had a missionary couple come through our church from Zambia one Sunday. As they told us about their ministry something welled up in me and my husband. We both felt compelled to make a large offering to them and then meet for a quick coffee. We weren't sure what would come from this but we committed it to prayer. My husband and I have always been very missions minded and we had already been to Central America several times. My husband was very instrumental in digging fresh water wells there. The following year I received a newsletter from the missionary couple in Zambia saying the Lord had given them the assignment for that year to be strategic in bringing in the harvest. When I read that my spirit leaped and the thought came, *I can help them do that!* Not really knowing for sure what that even looked like, I sent them an email saying that we would be willing to teach an evangelism course if they would have us. Their leadership team agreed and six months later we were in Kitwe, Zambia.

I was nervous and unsure who would even be in the class. As it turned out there were 19 people, 6 pastors each from a different denomination and the local missionaries. It was one of the most rewarding and life changing weeks of my life. Prior to us going there we had left our church of 25 years and were in a time of transition. I had been their worship leader and my husband was the sound man for 5 years but now I was no longer leading worship. I was trying to discover what this new season in my life would look like and I was starting to believe I had found it! The 19 people in the class, those called to full time ministry, even admitted they were not sharing the gospel enough. They were caught up in the day-to-day work and not focusing on what was the most important thing, saving souls!! The last day we all set out onto the streets putting into practice everything they had learned. The group consisted of some of the very boys the organization had rescued from the streets. They had come full circle and I was able to be a part of it. To God be the Glory!

When we came back to the states I was on cloud nine, but now what? I wanted to do more classes and to stir up, in the body of Christ, the passion to preach the gospel. I continued the small groups and offered to lead some local outreaches to the beach, which was a perfect training ground. I felt the call of an evangelist on me but was afraid to even call myself that. One day the Lord convicted me and told me *it's okay, this is your assignment, do it with boldness and do not be ashamed.*

I received a prophetic word from a prophetic minister, Tom Stamman, shortly after we returned from Africa. He confirmed the calling on my life and said he wanted to help me to make it happen! First of all, for a man to say to a woman *I want to help you develop one of the five fold ministry gifts* is rare. Operating in one of those roles as a woman is not always openly accepted. I felt the anointing to preach but had only been given a couple of opportunities in the past to do so. I always felt I was hitting a glass ceiling, that I was being held back, but not this time! Something ignited in my spirit and I had such a determination rise in me. I purposed in my heart to do what God told me to do and not wait for a church to acknowledge me and make it happen.

The first thing I did was to get ordained under Impact Ministries International. I then set up STW (Save The World) Ministries, which is our own 501(c)(3) nonprofit organization. Our vision is to help *save the world* one soul at a time. Our mission is to stir up a passion for preaching the gospel in the body of Christ through evangelism training workshops. We are willing to go anywhere in the world and teach practical ways of evangelism in non-confrontational and conversational ways.

Two years later the Lord gave me the idea of the Simple Gospel CD which is my worship and the word evangelistic tool. I share the gospel in and throughout music. The Father brought my two passions together, worship and the preaching of the gospel, into one project. It was not something I ever set out to do but God confirmed this idea by bringing not only divine inspiration, but the resources of money and the people to fulfill the vision. Over 1500 CD's have been distributed since November of 2017 and hundreds of digital downloads. He has used this project to touch people literally all over the world. To God be the glory because I can't take any credit but for saying yes!

[2]
THE TIME IS NOW

We must have a sense of urgency and not forget that none of us are promised tomorrow. The Bible *says today is the day of salvation*, people may not have another opportunity.

I know someone who is dying of an incurable cancer. His mortality is facing him and there is an urgency in my spirit to make sure he's right with God. When I asked him if he knows where he will go when he dies, he jokingly said, *I hope heaven, but I know I've been bad so God will probably make me go sit in a corner*. He laughed but under the facade I know he's not sure and he's thinking God is mad at him. I told him *you can be sure*, and I shared with him scriptures about God's love and forgiveness and that through repentance and accepting Jesus as his Savior he can inherit eternal life.

We need to have that same kind of urgency with

everyone God puts before us. Technically we all are dying, some just closer than others. It's time to strategically bring in the harvest and be purposeful in preaching the gospel. *2 Timothy 4:2 (AMP) Herald and preach the Word! Keep your sense of urgency [stand by, be at hand and ready], (whether the opportunity seems to be favorable or unfavorable, whether it is convenient or inconvenient, whether it is welcome or unwelcome.) Convince them, rebuking and correcting, warning and urging and encouraging them, being unflagging and inexhaustible in patience and teaching.*

Because of this urgency in my spirit to preach the good news, I started STW Ministries, Inc. and began this mission to teach others. I have observed and researched different methods of evangelism and have decided to develop my own curriculum using life experiences, various methodologies and teachings from some of the most notable evangelists and preachers. I have come to the conclusion that there is not just one way to evangelize. Every time I share my faith it looks a little different, because my audience is different. I find that if we only use one method, we can become too mechanical and lose the sensitivity to discern the Holy Spirit's direction. We need to be able to discern what the Spirit of God is wanting to communicate to the person. My goal is to provide believers with many different tools to hold in their evangelism tool belt.

Statically only 2% of Christians share their faith

regularly. 85% never invite anyone to church, and 95% never win anyone to Christ. Shocking isn't it, there's something wrong! We see all around us how Christianity is losing ground in the United States but what are we doing about it? We complain about how God is being removed from our government, our schools and workplaces. We need a righteous indignation to rise in our spirits and to let that become fuel to the fire. I want to challenge you to be the one who makes a difference and helps to change the statistics one soul at a time. *Matthew 9:37-38 (NIV) Then he said to his disciples, "The harvest is plentiful but the workers are few. Ask the Lord of the harvest, therefore, to send out the workers into His harvest field.*

I think we have developed some wrong mindsets and we expect the pastor, evangelist and others more spiritually mature to do all the work. But it's all of our responsibility because He has given us all authority to do so.

Matthew 28:18-20 (NIV) And Jesus came and said to them, 'all authority in heaven and on earth has been given to Me. Go therefore and make disciples of all nations, baptizing them in the Name of the Father and of the Son and of the Holy Spirit, teaching them to observe all that I have commanded you. And behold, I am with you always, to the end of the age.'

To share the gospel is to offer our account of His goodness and saving power. Sharing our faith and what He's done is to make the most out of our life. Jesus Christ saved and freed us to use us in this way. This is the business of heaven. To give out of what we have learned and make the way for another is one of life's greatest gifts! Why does the Bible say it is more blessed to give than to receive? Because it is out of the giving that we find joy and fulfillment knowing what we are doing is what we were created to do. Some of the most spiritually gratifying moments in my life are ministering to others the hope and promise of salvation. In fact, one of those healing and fruitful times of my life is when I worked in the Pro-Life movement. I was a volunteer counselor in a crisis pregnancy center for many years. It was my way of taking what the devil meant for evil and my destruction, and using it for good. Every time I was able to stop a woman from getting an abortion, I felt I had redeemed what I had done. It brought healing as I gave of myself, sharing my testimony and offering hope to the hurting women. I received so much more than what I felt I gave. Use the very things the devil has used against you and see it as your mission field. It gives you compassion and insight that others may not have. It's like saying, *"In your face devil!"*

Jesus commanded us in *Mark 16:15 (NIV) He said to them, "Go into all the world and preach the Good News to all creation.* We must ask ourselves, *what am I doing to expand the kingdom of God?* When was the last time I shared the Good News or discipled someone? If we can't remember the last time, we need to be concerned about the *sin of omission,* that is, *the things we know to do but don't do. James 4:17* (NLT) *Remember, it is sin to know what you ought to do and then not do it.* Whoa! It couldn't be clearer! We need to ask the Father to forgive us for not doing our part.

Every day we walk past people who are dying and going to hell and we don't do anything about it. If we had the cure for cancer would we withhold it from those who are sick? If we truly love people, we will take the time to do something about it. Do we think there really isn't a hell, or is it that we think they have plenty of time? The Apostle Paul said in *1 Cor. 9:16* (NIV) *For when I preach the gospel, I can not boast , since I am compelled to preach. Woe to me if I do not preach the gospel.* I do not mean to bring any condemnation on you, but to ignite something within you. *Hebrews 10:24 24 says, and let us consider how we may spur one another on toward love and good deeds.*

We must start living what we believe. Not just *sayers* but *doers* of the word. Billy Graham once said, *"We are the Bibles the world is reading. We are the creeds the world is needing; we are the sermons the world is heeding."* If we don't tell people about the treasure we have found why would they even want it if they know we are Christians but never found it valuable enough to share it with them? Do you have a favorite restaurant or movie that you tell everyone about? Could we get as excited about sharing Jesus as cheering for our favorite sports team or taking a stand for a political affiliation. It must start with a conviction, and then continue with the resolve to make it a priority and make it a part of our daily life.

> "Even if I were utterly selfish and had no care for anything but my own happiness, I would choose, if I might, under God, to be a soul winner, for never did I know perfect, overflowing, unutterable happiness of the purest and most ennobling order till I first heard of one who had sought and found a Savior through my means." —Charles Spurgeon

ACTION ITEMS:

Pray for forgiveness for the sin of omission, recognize if you have some wrong mindsets, and determine to be purposeful in being a witness for Christ.

[3]
BECOME UNSTOPPABLE

So, what is stopping you? We know as believers in Jesus we should be sharing our faith but why don't we? Could it be plain old fear, or that we just don't love people enough? The absence of love gives precedence to fear. Everything is subject to whether love is in operation or not. When faith operates in the presence of love, fear must flee.

So many Christians are not willing to take a stand for fear of being rejected or fear they will be called judgmental. There is a difference in how we approach people that can and will make all the difference. We can't stand on a street corner and scream at people to repent but we can engage people in spiritual conversations and plant the seeds of God's truth in love. This is my objective in this book, to debunk some wrong mindsets and make the presentation of the gospel to be nothing more than a *simple spiritual conversation.*

Is our fear of failure keeping us from stepping out? God is not just interested in the success of the witnessing opportunity, but in the act of obedience apart from the outcome. Every level of risk is rewarded equally regardless of the results! We must *do it afraid* as Joyce Meyer always says. The first time I approached a stranger in a popular shopping area, I walked past this man sitting on a bench 3 *times*.

I was so afraid to approach him, but when I finally gathered the courage to do so, it went very well. He engaged me in a conversation and he turned out to be a Christian. God gave me an easy one the first time! In fact he complimented me on my boldness in sharing the gospel. Maybe it wasn't just for my training but for him too. Maybe he needed to be reminded of the importance of preaching the good news as well. I have found it is not as scary as we play it out in our minds.

Fear is one of the devil's tools to stop us in our tracks. It can paralyze us from even trying. If we give in to fear, he wins! The Bible tells us over 80 times to fear not. *Isaiah 41:13 (NIV) says, For I am the Lord your God who takes hold of your right hand and says to you, Do not fear, I will help you.* What a promise from our Father! When God called me to Africa, I was afraid...but I pushed past my fears and the results were life changing. If I had not said yes, I would be missing out on all the great things the

Lord has done since then. Just the word *evangelism* seems to scare people away. I go to a large church and whenever I conduct one of my evangelism training classes, percentage wise, I have very few who sign up. Yet any class about self-improvement, the classes are full. What's all the self improvement good for if we don't use it?

James 2:17 (NLT) So you see, faith by itself isn't enough. Unless it produces good deeds, it is dead and useless. We can become like stagnant water if we don't allow the flow of His spiritual gifts to pass through us. We are a conduit of His love, grace and mercy. I will never forget when the Lord spoke to my heart, *if the blessings ever stop flowing through you like a conduit, the anointing will also stop.* I took heed to that warning! I don't ever want to become a stagnant cesspool.

There is a cost to the anointing and that cost is our selfish flesh! We are blessed to be a blessing not be a hoarder of knowledge and spiritual gifts. We need to allow the living water to flow through us and onto to others. We have become too self-absorbed and it creates depressed and unhappy Christians. If you are finding yourself being critical and a "Debbie Downer" start looking for opportunities to serve and minister to others and watch that kind of attitude start to disappear. When we start looking at the needs of others more than ourselves, we start to minimize the things that made us so unhappy in the first place.

One of the ways to combat fear is being confident in who we are in Christ. I believe we would not need all the self-help and deliverance ministry if we truly understood who we are in Christ. Our identity is not our title and what we do but who we are as children of the Most High God and disciples of Christ. There was a time in my life when I felt my identity was being a worship leader. So, when I stepped down and we left our church of 25 years because God told us that it was time to leave the nest...I felt lost. It was hard for me to leave my role because I so loved leading people into God's presence. I thought I would just start leading worship again at another church. I was mistaken.

He purposely placed us in a church that didn't quite fit my style of worship and made me be still and not serve for a time. Well my type A, do'er personality had a hard time with that and I can be a little hard headed. I joined their worship team but very quickly knew it was like pounding a square peg into a round hole. Obedience is better than sacrifice the Bible says! During that two year transition period God stripped away some wrong mindsets and reminded me who I really was, a child of God, and that my identity was not in what I did for him.

He spoke to my heart, "Will you worship Me in obscurity? If you never have a platform again will you still worship me?" I just broke down in tears and said, *of course I will!* I asked for forgiveness and had a renewed sense of my worth in Him. He wants us to do good things for the kingdom, but it's really our heart He's after. We must always keep that in perspective and check that our motives are pure. *Timothy 1:5 (NIV) The goal of this command is love, which comes from a pure heart and a good conscience and a sincere faith.*

We must keep our relationship with Jesus a priority. Everything flows out of the intimacy we have with Him. That is where we get our sense of identity and assurance of His unconditional love which helps us to overcome our fears. We are His workmanship, He delights in us and He desires for us to commune with Him and to be near to His heart.

Unrealistic expectations are another stumbling block to sharing our faith. We put too much pressure on ourselves for the outcome. Don't take on a false sense of responsibility. It is freeing when you take the pressure off of yourself and realize you haven't failed just because you weren't able to lead someone through the sinner's prayer. I used to really have a problem with this. I would feel I didn't do a good enough job if it didn't lead to them praying to receive Christ. But then I got the revelation that the Holy Spirit is the One that brings the conviction which leads to the ultimate confession of faith. I am just to make myself available to be used by God and He will do the rest. We are co-laborers with Christ. *1 Cor. 3:7 (NLT) It's not important who does the planting or who does the watering. What's important is that God makes the seed grow.*

We are either *sowing* or *watering* gospel seeds. If the Lord makes it evident that it is time for increase, well then, awesome for the privilege to lead someone to Christ at that moment, but either way, we're all part of the process. The Bible says to be ready in and out of season and to have an answer for the joy in your heart. Peter makes this statement in *1 Peter 3:15-16 (NASB) sanctify Christ as Lord in your hearts, always being ready to make a defense to everyone who asks you to give an account for the hope that is in you, yet with gentleness and reverence; and keep a good conscience so that in the thing in which you are slandered, those who revile your good behavior in Christ may be put to shame.* We have a responsibility to keep ourselves blameless so people won't have an excuse to not believe because of our bad witness. We want to draw them to Christ and not do anything to push them away. I can't stress this enough, too many people have been turned away from Christ because of someone's bad witness.

Maybe the problem is you feel unqualified? Many unqualified men and women of the Bible had fears and insecurities. God qualifies the unqualified and He uses the foolish things to confound the wise. Moses said to the Lord, "Oh, my Lord, I am not eloquent, either in the past or since you have spoken to your servant, but I am slow of speech and of tongue." Gideon said, "Please, Lord, how can I save Israel? Behold, my clan is the weakest in Manasseh, and I am the least in my father's house." And look what these men did for God? They were just like us, no different. I found the times I'm on the edge of myself are the times I really dig into the Bible and depend on the Holy Spirit. I love to feel the presence of God in me in those moments. There is nothing else like it.

One of those times, I was ministering on the beach and I was speaking with a group of college age guys. Approaching a group of strangers can be intimidating yet I pushed through my fear and obeyed the voice of God. God gave me a specific word for each one of them. They couldn't believe how accurate the things I was saying about them were. It not only built my faith in trusting God to work through me, but it was undeniable that the power of God was at work! They thanked me for the encouraging words and I left feeling so grateful that I said *yes*. We will talk later in the book about the power of the prophetic word. Do you say to yourself, *I don't have all the right words or know how to say them?*

When God called Jeremiah to be a prophet, He spoke to him in *Jeremiah 1:4-10 (ESV) The word of the Lord came to me, saying, 'Before I formed you in the womb I knew you, and before you were born I consecrated you; I appointed you a prophet to the nations.' Then I said, 'Ah, Lord God! Behold, I do not know how to speak, for I am only a youth.' But the Lord said to me, 'Do not say, 'I am only a youth'; for to all to whom I send you, you shall go, and whatever I command you, you shall speak. Do not be afraid of them, for I am with you to deliver you, declares the Lord." Then the Lord put out His hand and touched my mouth. And the Lord said to me, 'Behold, I have put My words in your mouth. See, I have set you this day over nations and kingdoms, to pluck up and to break down, to destroy and to overthrow, to build and to plant.'* God is not looking for the qualified but rather for the ones who will make themselves available. He wants us to be totally dependent on Him. When we are stretched beyond our comfort zone it puts a demand on our faith and makes us dig a little deeper and press in a little harder. If we don't ever put ourselves in situations that stretch us, we'll never grow.

The root of this unwillingness to step out is pride. We worry more about our reputation than making His Name known. We all want people to like us and we don't want to look foolish, but being a people pleaser is a trap and can be a vicious cycle. We all struggle with this from time to time, some more than others. We must ask ourselves, what is the level of risk I am taking for Him? Is it higher than my desire for success or popularity? We need to recognize how fear of man may have a hold on our mind. It is a controlling spirit! I hate the feeling when I knew I should speak and didn't! What's the worst thing that could happen. I look at it as: *it is better to try than to never try at all.* Bottom line is we need to be willing to get over the view others have of us and to care more about pleasing God.

Grace is God's unmerited favor and gives us our

strength and ability to do the supernatural. When we get away from focusing on our own inadequacies and weaknesses and focus more on the work of the Holy Spirit in us, we can overcome those feelings. 2 *Cor. 12:9 (ESV) But he said to me, 'My grace is sufficient for you, for my power is made perfect in weakness.' Therefore I will boast all the more gladly of my weaknesses, so that the power of Christ may rest upon me.*

This is so opposite of what the world thinks. The world view is *be strong don't admit your weaknesses.* By admitting our weaknesses, it makes us stronger in *His* might. If that doesn't take the pressure off, I don't know what does!

Jesus talks about how in the last days the hearts of many will grow cold. (see Matthews 24) . I believe that is what we are witnessing today in our society as we enter the last days before Jesus Christ returns. I also believe this scripture is talking about many in the church and not just society as a whole. We expect the world to be cold but not the church. We need to have more compassion for people and what happens to them. Matthew 19 says to *love thy neighbor as thyself.* That's a tall order and yet God asks us to display this selfless type of love. We can't possibly love in this way on our own, we need to pray for the *agape* type of love for people and for our hearts to break with the things that break God's heart. The love that compels us to go beyond ourselves and do anything to save another is what is lacking in this world.

1 Corinthians 13:4-8 (NIV) Love is patient, love is kind. It does not envy, it does not boast, it is not proud. It does not dishonor others, it is not self-seeking, it is not easily angered, it keeps no record of wrongs. Love does not delight in evil but rejoices with the truth. It always protects, always trusts, always hopes, always perseveres.

I believe one of the things that sabotages 1st Corinthians type of love is being prejudiced against different types of people. It keeps us at a distance. You may be saying, *well I'm not* prejudice *in any way,* but if you really think about it, we can all have certain people we have decided we don't want to associate with. We have to see people as God sees them. He desires that all would be saved. We can also take offense and build a wall around us so people can't hurt or offend us again. We need to push past the exterior and see the broken person within. *Hurting people hurt people.*

I had a situation in my family where a family member said some very hurtful things about my mom and brother. I was very angry and wanted to retaliate. There was a family wedding coming up and so I prayed for God to give me love for this person. Everything in me didn't want to do it but I did it anyways. When I saw this person at the wedding I was overwhelmed with love for her, I hugged her and told her how happy I was that she was there. *Colossians 3:13-14 (NIV) Bear with each other and forgive one another if any of you has a grievance against someone. Forgive as the LORD forgave you. And over all these virtues put on love, which binds them all together in perfect unity.*

We often hear, *take the high road and be the better person,* which is so true. I know it is easier said than done but God can give us the grace to do it. When we respond in that way it builds in us *Christlike character*, which is the ultimate goal. I often say to myself, *I must decrease so Christ can increase.* Our prejudice and offense against people will stop us from loving and forgiving and doing the things we know we should. Don't allow excuses to stop you from demonstrating Christ's love for people. You may say, *I've asked them to church already and they won't come or what's the use, it won't really matter. They are too mean and too far gone and I'm done!*

I'm not saying to be a doormat for people, but we can't give up on people too quickly. There are times when God will say *move on,* but until He does, be persistent. I know I'm so glad Jesus never gave up on me and kept pursuing me! Life can be messy and painful, and I believe that is what Paul meant in Romans 5 when he talked about sharing in Christ's glory and His suffering. That long suffering produces far more character in us than the glory part! *Romans 5:3 Not only so, but we also glory in our sufferings, because we know that suffering produces perseverance; perseverance, character; and character, hope.*

As disciples of Christ we must know His Word so we know how to speak His truths accurately. Just picking up our Bible on Sundays is not going to cut it. *Romans 10:17 says, Faith comes by hearing and hearing the word of God.* We must get the truth of God's words deep in our hearts. Speak it out loud so your spirit and mind can be strengthened and built up. We need to study the Word of God and be an *ever learning student* of what it teaches us so we properly communicate it to others. Memorize John 3:16 and other key scriptures I'll be sharing with you. *2 Timothy 2:15 (NASB) Be diligent to present yourself approved to God as a workman who does not need to be unashamed, accurately* handling the *word of truth.*

That doesn't mean we have to quote scripture word for word and remember the verse number to speak the word of truth. But we must know how to wield our mighty sword! Unbelievers don't know the difference if we don't quote it just perfectly. What they really want to know is that you care, and you are sincere. Love and sincerity can go a long way and it is the core of the gospel message. Many people feel unloved and don't have someone to encourage and pray for them. The gift of encouragement is so underused and undervalued. It is a powerful gift and can speak life into a weary soul. Proverbs 11:25 says, *those who refresh others will be refreshed themselves.* Do you need some refreshing today? Go look for someone to bless and encourage. They are everywhere so you will not have to look hard!

God doesn't need us but He gives us the awesome opportunity to be His hands and feet and demonstrate

His love for people. Telling them that Jesus loves them and what He did for them can help people feel loved and valued. It can soften a hardened heart. I prayed for this woman one time in my office that was so agitated and upset but by the time I finished praying her demeanor completely changed. The thieves of *religion* and *false doctrines* are out to kill, steal and destroy us, but Jesus came that we may have life and have it in abundance! John 10:10.

ACTION ITEMS:

Ask the Lord what you fear and why? Give it to Him. What is the thing He has been asking you to do, but you haven't done it because you feel unqualified? Write it down and commit it to prayer and take action.

[4]
HAPPINESS VS. RIGHTEOUSNESS GOSPEL

Jesus did not come for happiness sake but righteousness' sake. He came to save us from the wrath of God by providing a way for us to have right standing with him, not just for life improvement. *John 3:36 Whoever believes in the Son has eternal life, but whoever rejects the Son will not see life, for God's wrath remains on them.*

The happiness gospel can create a lot of *mushroom converts*. Because of the stony ground that the seeds were sown into (no conviction of the law/sin) they receive the word with joy but at the first sign of tribulation, temptation or persecution they fall away. For many years I shared the *happiness gospel*. It was much easier to tell people that Jesus will give them a wonderful, beautiful life but it was not the full gospel, it was a half-truth. Yes, happiness is a byproduct of Christianity, but it should not be the reason people come to Christ. The real reason He came was to offer us eternal life! We are to tell *the whole truth and nothing but the truth, so help us God!!* How many times have we heard that, but it's so true of the gospel. We are doing people a disservice if we sell the gospel as if it's a *get happy quick* scheme. We have Americanized the gospel and made it more palatable. If we sell people on the idea to come to Jesus for a wonderful beautiful life, it's an easier sale than addressing sin, repentance and living a holy life acceptable and pleasing to God. We end up with *decision makers* and not true *disciples*. We don't want people to expect God to be like their *sugar daddy* that gives them everything they want when they want it. If people come to Jesus on that premise and things don't go their way, they give up on God and can become a hardened critic. Most people have sown bad seeds and are reaping the consequences and it takes time to turn things around and start sowing good seeds that produce good fruit.

I believe that for way too long evangelism has gotten a bad rap. Many Christians don't preach the gospel because they think they'll be associated with the fanatical person standing on the street corner screaming and waving a Bible in the air telling people they are going to hell. So, like most instances, the pendulum swings too far in the opposite direction and now there is no mention of hell or judgment, only God's promise of a better life here on earth. However, if you look at the disciple's lives, it was not an easy life. It was a life filled with persecution,

HAPPINESS VS. RIGHTEOUSNESS GOSPEL / 33

pain, and many hardships. Jesus said, *I have said these things to you, that in Me you may have peace. In the world you will have tribulation. But take heart; I have overcome the world. John 16:33 (ESV)* Through it all they had a peace and conviction of who Jesus was and why He came. They were driven by eternity!

So why doesn't the life enrichment/wonderful plan for your life work? Because too many Christians walk away from Christianity because they came to Christ for the wrong reasons. They try it out and see how it works for them instead of having a deep conviction they are sinners in need of a Savior. I heard this analogy from Ray Comfort that so clearly demonstrates how we can sell the *happiness gospel* message. It goes like this. There was a flight across the Atlantic and as passengers boarded the plane they were told to put on a parachute because it would improve the flight. The passengers soon learned the parachute was uncomfortable and some of the passengers that didn't put one on were laughing at them. In frustration and feeling a little deceived, they took off the parachute and threw it to the ground vowing to never do that again.

Now on the next flight the flight attendant gave the passengers a different reason to wear the parachute. As the passengers boarded, the flight attendant told them to put on the parachute because they would be flying at 30,000 feet and if the plane were to go down it would save their life. This time *all* the passengers put on the parachute and as the plane incurred some rough turbulence, they clung even tighter to the parachute knowing it would save their life. See the difference in how people perceived and responded to the parachute. If we tell people that Jesus will solve all their problems and then their marriage fails and they still go through divorce or someone still dies they will not appreciate what they were given and possibly be worse off. We can inoculate them, and they may never return to Christ. *2 Peter 2:21 (NLT) It would be better if they had never known the way to righteousness than to know it and then reject the command they were given to live a holy life.*

I'm not talking about people who may backslide from time to time, but I hope you hear my heart in this. I was one of those people who put on the rose-colored glasses and wasn't living for righteousness sake and so when the evil tempted me and things got shaky I caved! I didn't realize how sin desensitizes our spirit and we don't hear His voice. It can harden our hearts and make it so that we don't live to please God because we would rather live to please ourselves. It's a lie to believe we can be saved, continue to sin and live in abundance. God will always love us but living in continual sin separates us from Him and we will suffer consequences.

As I learned more about how to share the full gospel and what Jesus preached I wanted to not only learn this for myself and my family but for others. That's why I started holding small groups where I would teach others what I had learned and what led to the writing of this book. I wish someone would have prepared me better and I would have had this understanding early on. That's why the full gospel must be presented, we don't want people to be misled. The other point that really convicted me about selling the *happiness gospel* was the challenge of talking to someone who is already happy, has plenty of money and no problems. Then what do I offer them? The gospel is not for just the down and out. It is the same gospel message no matter the ethnicity, financial status, age or culture. It does not discriminate. I must be able to preach the same gospel message everywhere in the world to anybody.

ACTION ITEMS:

Recognize if you have been selling the "happiness gospel" and commit to preaching the whole truth. Write out a gospel presentation that accurately explains the *righteousness* centered gospel and prepare to share it with someone God puts on your heart.

[5]
THE LAW'S PURPOSE

So what is the purpose of the law today? *Romans 3:19-20 (NLT) Obviously, the law applies to those to whom it was given, for its purpose is to keep people from having excuses, and to show that the entire world is guilty before God. For no one can ever be made right with God by doing what the law commands.*

The law simply shows us how sinful we are. We clearly see we are not justified by the law, but the law only shows us our humanity and sin. We cannot forsake the use of the law of God and its ability to lead a sinner to the cross and repentance. Jesus used the law to make people realize they sinned and so should we. The Bible says everyone is born with a conscience and a deep-down feeling of what is right and wrong. *Romans 2:15 (NLT) They demonstrate that God's law is written in their hearts, for their own conscience and thoughts either accuse them or tell them they are doing right.* Let the law of God and a person's conscience do the work to bring conviction. You are only the messenger and if they have an issue, they can take it up with the Lord. In fact, that is when I say, *don't just take my word for it, read the Bible for yourselves and discover what it says.* We want to keep pointing them to Jesus Christ and help them discover what the word of God says. So many people debate things they have no understanding of.

"The unsaved are in no condition to receive the gospel until the Law be applied to their hearts. It is a waste of time to sow seed on ground which has never been ploughed. To present the sacrifice of Christ to those whose dominant passion is to sin is to give what is holy to the dogs." —A.W. Pink

The cross seems foolish to people if they don't understand the *why* behind Christ's death. They are blind to their sin until you make them realize they have a *sin problem*. They don't understand their need for a Savior and that He is the answer to the sin problem. Christ came to fulfill the Law not to do away with it.

Matt 5:17-20 (NLT) Don't misunderstand why I have come. I did not come to abolish the law of Moses or the writings of the prophets. No, I came to accomplish their purpose. I tell you the truth, until heaven and earth disappear, not even the smallest detail of God's law will disappear until its purpose is achieved. So if you ignore the least commandment and teach others to do the same, you will be called the least in the Kingdom of Heaven. But anyone who obeys God's laws and teaches them will be called great in the Kingdom of Heaven. But I warn you— unless your righteousness is better than the righteousness of the teachers of religious law and the Pharisees, you will never enter the Kingdom of Heaven! Father God knew we could not live up to the Law so that is why He sent Jesus to free us from the bondage of the law of sin and death.

I'll never forget when one of my kids said, *we don't have to follow the 10 commandments anymore mom.* I was surprised and thought *how did he come to that conclusion.* I'm afraid many think this way, and I think that is why sin is rampant in the church today. Also because we don't have a healthy fear and reverence for God. We can't just look at God as our Buddy, He is a holy and righteous judge and we must give Him reverence and honor. *Proverbs 14:27 (NIV) The fear of the Lord is a fountain of life, that one may turn away from the snares of death.* The bible also says that, *the fear of the Lord is the beginning of wisdom (Proverbs 9:10).* It's fundamental in how we perceive and respond to God.

It's called HYPER GRACE when we believe we can live in unrepentant sin and that we don't have to live by such a high standard of the 10 Commandments anymore. We think we can get away with it because we are forgiven anyway and the blood of Jesus covers us. We are abusing the grace of God and taking it for granted. He will forgive those who repent but there will be consequences! Sin is incredibly expensive and not in cash but paid in mental, emotional and spiritual pain. Sin is our defiant rejection of truth with an effort to satisfy our own selfish desires. We can not ride the fence between serving God and the world. We can not serve two masters! Righteous living is a choice and we can't underestimate the importance. Jesus said, *be holy as I am holy* in *1 Peter 1:16*. Living pure and holy doesn't mean we're perfect it means that we are only in a pursuit to be pure. *We do not want to do anything that will grieve the Holy Spirit of God that is within us Ephesians 4:30* (PARA). He sees everything!

The Ten Commandments in Exodus 20:3-17 are our guidelines and set the standard. He didn't give us an arbitrary list of *Do's and Dont's* just to see if we could follow them, no he laid out guidelines to protect us. Notice the first 4 commandments are commandments to honor God and the last 6 are to honor each other. We see the summation of these commandments in Matthew 22: 36-40 (NIV) when the disciples asked Jesus, *"Teacher, which is the greatest commandment in the Law? Jesus replied 'Love the Lord your God with all your heart and with all your soul and with all your mind. This is the first and greatest commandment. And the second is like it: 'Love your neighbor as yourself. All the Law and the Prophets hang on these two commandments.'"*

They are *commandments*, not just suggestions to live

by. They still have merit and help us reap the promises of God. Every promise of God comes with a condition that must be executed on our part. It's a collaboration of the sovereignty of God and the responsibility of man at work.

1. You shall have no other gods before Me (put God first above all)
2. You shall not make for yourself an idol (make a god to suit yourself))
3. You shall not misuse the Name of the Lord your God (blasphemy and use God's name in vain)
4. Remember the Sabbath Day by keeping it holy
5. Honor your father and mother
6. You shall not murder (same as hate)
7. You shall not commit adultery (even lust is considered adultery)
8. You shall not steal
9. You shall not give false testimony (lie)
10. You shall not covet (jealousy and greed)

There needs to be a healthy balance between Law and Grace. Because, if we put too much emphasis on law we can become legalistic and it can become all about trying to follow all the rules which is religion. With the Law we break hardened self-righteous hearts, and the gospel of grace is given to the broken and humble. Law to the proud and grace to the humble, two approaches, the same gospel message with a different emphasis. We are not saved by the law, the law only chases us to Calvary.

Gal 3: 24 (KJV) Wherefore the law was our schoolmaster to bring us unto Christ, that we might be justified by faith. The law and the word of truth can force them to their knees where then the love of Jesus can meet them. *Psalm 51:17 (NIV) My sacrifice, O God, is a broken spirit; a broken and contrite heart you, God, will not despise.*

People need a revelation of how much God hates sin and that He cannot allow a sinner to enter heaven. So often people will say God is too good to send people to hell. I use the analogy of the courtroom in these situations. Imagine you are a witness in a court of law. A man comes before the judge shackled in chains who has committed a heinous crime. The man pleads for his life and says I'm sorry and I'll never do it again. If the judge lets him go just because he apologized and said he would never do it again, what would you think of that judge? He would not be a good judge at all. Whereas God, who is a God of love is also a righteous judge and He must judge our sin. No matter how sorry we are. I believe this is where we as humans can miss it. We categorize sin whereas sin is sin in the eyes of God, no sin worse than another. The only way we can be set free is by accepting the price Jesus Christ paid for our transgressions. We must believe that He is the Son of God who willingly died on a cross, shed His blood, and rose on the third day...only then can we be forgiven and have eternal life.

Someone who is already humbled and hungry for truth, you can go straight to the Good News. We need to explain that it is by faith and the free gift of grace, which is *the unmerited favor of God,* that we can receive Him, and not by our good works. *Eph. 2:8-9 (ESV) For by grace you have been saved through faith. And this is not your own doing; it is the gift of God, not a result of works, so that no one may boast.* They can come as they are with no fear or condemnation. For these people, convincing them they *are worth Jesus dying for* will be the hardest thing, because at this point they usually are at a place of feeling lost and unworthy. Proving to them how much Jesus knows them, loves them and desires to have a personal relationship with them will be very important. Of course, they still need to understand what the "standard" is and the importance of righteous living, but the law is not required to show them they are a sinner—they already know that. They need to understand the Law is an expression of God's character and we are to represent that character ourselves as believers in Jesus Christ.

ACTION ITEMS:

Start a list of 5 people you want to share the full gospel with and as we continue through the book find the different tools that will work best for each one.

[6]
WITNESSING TO THE GOOD PERSON

Just because someone goes to church or is a good person doesn't mean they will go to heaven. We will know them by their fruit (the fruit of the Spirit) the Bible says in *Matthew 7:16 (PARA) If you are a rain cloud you rain, if you are an apple tree, we should see some apples!* Many people are quick to say they are a Christian but if there is no evidence of that fact, they may be deceived.

Matt. 7:21-23 (NLT) Not everyone who calls out to me, 'Lord! Lord!' will enter the Kingdom of Heaven. Only those who actually do the will of my Father in heaven will enter. On judgment day many will say to me, 'Lord! Lord! We prophesied in your name and cast out demons in your name and performed many miracles in your name. But I will reply, 'I never knew you. Get away from me, you who break God's law.

This is a very sobering scripture and we need to

realize that there will be a separation between the sheep and the goats. We may all be in the same pen, *i.e. the church,* but we are not *all going to heaven.* Some are wolves in sheep's clothing or they carry a Pharisee Spirit and are very carnal. We are not to judge the condition of someone's heart because that is between them and God. I'm just saying we can't always assume they are truly saved. So often when I ask people if they know where they will go when they die, they will say *I'm going to heaven,* and when I ask them how they know, they answer *because I'm a good person. Proverbs* 20:6 (PARA) says *every man will claim his own goodness.* Others will say hesitantly, I think I'll go to heaven but I'm not sure. That tells me a lot about their theology.

If they think they must be *good enough* or *earn their way* they will always doubt their salvation. That is *religion* and many have been led astray by believing this. We can be sure and we have the blessed assurance. *John 6:47-48 (NIV) Very truly I tell you, the one who believes in me has eternal life. I am the bread of life.*

The word *believe* in Hebrew means much more than just believe, for even the devil believes in Jesus. The word *believe* is the very same Hebrew verb *aman.* The Hebrew word translated as "firm" here is the verb which literally means "to be firm or sure". The picture we have from this is that Abram was firm in his devotion to God. Just as a stake planted in firm ground supports the tent, even in a storm, Abram stood firm for God, even in the storms of life and it was credited to him as righteousness.

We cannot work our way into heaven by our good works but only by believing and trusting in Jesus as Savior to save and redeem us. *2 Corinthians 5:21 (NIV) For our sake he made him to be sin who knew no sin, so that in him we might become the righteousness of God.* It is our job to communicate this truth to those who may rely on their *religion* and *checking all the right boxes* to inherit eternal life.

God has a very high standard, nowhere close to our idea of what is good. The target is the glory of God, the Greek word for glory is *doxa*, which means *honor, worship, praise*. Humanity has fallen short of God's mark by failing to give our Creator the honor, worship and praise due Him. We have failed to love God with all our heart, mind, soul and strength, which is the essence of the first commandment.

In fact, the statement *all have sinned* comes in the context of the Apostle Paul saying that the Law has left the whole world guilty before God. *Romans 3:23 (NIV) for all have sinned and fall short of the glory of God.* The Law is the target, the standard by which our best shot will be measured. If we fail to tell people anything about the mark which we are aiming for, we leave them believing that they can simply give it their best shot.

However, when we display the high standard of the Law, we show them the utter hopelessness of them ever coming close! Their only hope then is in the Savior. Convicted sinners are left with a dilemma: Now what? Only then are they ready to hear and receive the gospel message of salvation through Jesus Christ, because only then do they realize how lost and off the mark they truly are! How can sinners be brought to true repentance and thus true salvation if they don't realize this very important fact. If they don't we will continue to witness the devastating results.

Romans 7:13 (AMP) *Did that which is good [the Law], then become death to me? Certainly not! But sin, in order that it might be revealed as sin, was producing death in me by [using] this good thing [as a weapon], so that through the commandment sin would become exceedingly sinful.*

Let's look at how Ray Comfort and Kirk Cameron, authors and teachers of *the Way of the Master* use what they call Hell's Best Kept Secret (use of the 10 commandments) in conversation. Mr. John Do Good, I have come to realize there is a big difference between God's standard verses man's standard of good. I consider myself to be a good person but also realized I can never be good enough to gain access to heaven. As hard as I try to always do good I somehow still fail short.

May I ask you a few questions that I've had to ask myself, and share with you the solution to this dilemma?

- Would you consider yourself to be a good person?
- Do you think you have kept the 10 Commandments? (Mention a few of the 10 Commandments)
- If God were to judge you by the 10 Commandments do you think you would be innocent or guilty?
- Do you think you would go to heaven or hell?
- Does that concern you?
- Do you want to know how you can be forgiven and have eternal life?

Once you get their reply to these questions present the solution, the gospel message!

- Jesus suffered for our sins, died on a cross and rose on the third day
- Confess, repent and forsake all sin
- Trust in Jesus as your Lord and Savior
- Point to these truths in the Bible and encourage them to get right with God today.
- Guide them in a prayer of salvation

By asking these few questions people may come to realize they are not *as good as they think they are* compared to God's standard. Now you will have some discussion among these questions, but just try and follow the main points. What you eventually want to see occur, before you share the good news of the Gospel, is for them to stop trying to make excuses.

For them to stop playing the, *but I'm a good person* card and have a look of conviction and humility. Then you can give them the solution, which is Jesus our Savior who came to save us from the wrath of God. *Mal.2:6 (AMS) The law of truth was in his mouth, and unrighteousness was not found in his lips: he walked with me in peace and uprightness, and turned many away from iniquity.*

ACTION ITEMS:

Use this dialogue with one of the people on your Top 5 List who claims to be the "Good Person"

[7]
TREASURE HUNTING

TREASURE HUNTING IS AN OUTREACH ACTIVITY THAT is all about being led by the Holy Spirit as you go out and minister to people. Jesus left this earth so the Holy Spirit could come and be our guide and helper. *John 16:7-8 (NLT) But in fact, it is best for you that I go away, because if I don't, the Advocate won't come. If I do go away, then I will send him to you. And when he comes, he will convict the world of its sin, and of God's righteousness, and of the coming judgment.*

I have some very fond memories of taking a youth group treasure hunting. We would sit quietly before the Lord with paper and pen in hand and ask Him for clues. The first things that pop into our heads we write down, such as names, attributes, places, colors etc. any word that would come to mind. Then we would set out to the streets in search of these clues. With clues in hand it helps you to target and be more strategic in whom to approach out of the many people you come across.

We believed God was going to set us up for some divine appointments. Sure enough, He did. We would tell people that we were a local youth group out praying for people and then ask permission to pray for them. We would show them our clues so they would know why we chose them. Many times, people were excited by the fact that God would highlight them. I had one situation where one of my clues was white high-top tennis shoes.

Well there we were in a Big Lots store and sitting in a recliner was this gang looking guy and he had on white high-top tennis shoes. It was as if those shoes were glowing! As I approached him and told him who and why we were there he got all excited. He said he had just recently been released from prison and he was wanting to get his life right with God! We shared the gospel and prayed for him and he was very appreciative. If I had not had that clue I would not have stopped and spoken to him. The rest of the day went about the same. Everyone was not only surprised, because it's so unexpected, but thankful. Many people don't ever experience the laying on of hands and being prayed for. They can feel the power of God through our prayers and are often moved to tears.

Supernatural encounters, love and kindness, rather than arguments and debates, win people to Christ. Using the prophetic gifts expressed in *words of knowledge* (information obtained by the Holy Spirit) can be the key to unlock a heart. *Words of knowledge* are an effective resource available to believers. This is a powerful tool and is so misunderstood and underused because I believe too many think it is a gift for only the chosen few. Well I beg to differ, because that is not what the Word says.

1 Cor. 14: 1-5 (NLT) Let love be your highest goal! But you should also desire the special abilities the Spirit gives—especially the ability to prophesy. For if you have the ability to speak in tongues, you will be talking only to God, since people won't be able to understand you. You will be speaking by the power of the Spirit, but it will all be mysterious. But one who prophesies strengthens others, encourages them, and comforts them. A person who speaks in tongues is strengthened personally, but one who speaks a word of prophecy strengthens the entire church. I wish you could all speak in tongues, but even more I wish you could all prophesy.

When we ask God for the spiritual gifts of the Spirit, He will give them to us. If we ask Father for bread would he give us a stone? Of course not, because He loves to bless his children with all spiritual blessings. I believe we just need a better understanding and knowledge of the subject. We must ask for the gifts by faith, believe we receive and then exercise our gifts. Practicing our ability to hear and act on that *still small voice is essential for the development of that gift*. When I first started to operate in my prophetic gift I received literal physical feelings. I think God did this because He wanted me not to mistake whether it was Him or not. Often the words would build up in my chest and I would feel as if I was going to explode if I didn't let them out! There have been so many times when I have spoken what I felt God wanted to say to someone and they would confirm it by saying, "how did you know that?" or "that is exactly what I've been feeling."

Whenever we step out in faith there is always fruit that come from it. Let me share with you a recent story of God using me to speak to a young girl who did not believe in God but was willing for me to pray for her. As I was praying the Lord gave me words of knowledge about her that I included in my prayer. When we finished she was shocked I knew of these things. I told her I was a Christian and that God was using me to speak to her to remind her that He knows her, loves her and wants to reveal Himself to her. She couldn't wait to tell her friend what happened because her friend had been trying to get her to church. I was able to plant a seed by demonstrating the power and presence of God which was hopefully enough to then push her to church. Will you be the one who will say "Yes, Lord speak through me!" You will be so glad you did because your life will never be the same!

If we believe God hears us when we pray, why don't we have that same faith to believe we can hear from Him and speak on His behalf? Our thoughts can be His thoughts through the power of the Spirit. Our carnal nature doesn't want to bless, encourage or do any good thing, it is only the Holy Spirit within us that compels us to do good. That is a sign in itself that it is the prompting of the Holy Spirit. *Romans 12:2 (ESV) Do not be conformed to this world, but be transformed by the renewal of your mind, that by testing you may discern what is the will of God, what is good and acceptable and perfect.* Learning to tap into this *new mind* and discern that you are hearing from God takes time to develop. I think of it as *fine tuning a radio station*. At first it's all static, but then as you *dial in* you hear that clear frequency. Each time you give a word and it's confirmed by someone, you will learn to trust it and recognize it more quickly the next time.

Allow me to provide you with a few guidelines when it comes to prophesying to someone. Only use the prophetic to bless, encourage and for the common good. You never use it to embarrass or condemn. Tell people "I believe this is what the Lord is saying" or "I feel God is saying this or that." You are human and you can and will miss it, but if you stay within the guidelines, to encourage and not condemn, you will still leave the person feeling uplifted. It's always good to have another person present. Never tell people something that would cause them to make a major life decision, i.e. marry someone, move to a specific place, quit a job. You get the picture. It must always line up with the Word of God and be biblically sound.

Let's look at the way the Lord Jesus witnessed to the

woman at the well in John 4:1-42. Notice the steps He made using the Law and the prophetic gift.

- First, He took a conversation from the natural to the spiritual when He asked her for a drink and then He used the analogy of *living water* that she would no longer thirst.
- He built a bridge by extending hospitality. It was considered taboo for Jews to associate with Samaritans, and with a woman on top of that!
- He demonstrated His power through the prophetic knowledge He had about her having five previous husbands.
- He used the law and referenced the 7th Commandment, *do not commit adultery*. She realized her sin and it brought conviction.
- He didn't promise a wonderful plan for her life, He only promised to be her Savior.
- She believed, and her testimony then convinced others.

This is the perfect witnessing scenario and if it worked for Jesus, we should use this as our model as well. You're probably thinking right now *but that was Jesus who am I to do the same as Jesus did.* Because we have the same Spirit and we can walk in the same power and authority. *Acts 1:8 (NIV) But you will receive power when the Holy Spirit has come upon you, and you will be my witnesses in Jerusalem and in all Judea and Samaria, and to the end of the earth."*

ACTION ITEMS:

Do the Treasure Hunting exercise with some friends, a home group or youth group, to not only do outreach together but to stretch and strengthen your faith and exercise your prophetic gift.

[8]
WITNESSING TO FAMILY AND FRIENDS

STATISTICS SHOW THAT 79% OF CHRISTIANS COME TO Christ through a friend or relative. I believe this is the case because there is a basis of trust already established with most of these people. Yet we are afraid to challenge their way of thinking if it is contrary to God's Word regarding why Jesus came to earth and their eternity. I believe it's because we are afraid we may lose a friend or aggravate a family member. Most of us avoid confrontation like the plague. However, I would propose that we not look at it as *confrontation* but a level of *accountability* and *teaching others God's truth about their salvation.*

Proverbs 28:23 says (AMP) He who rebukes a man shall afterward find more favor than he who flatters with the tongue. Flattery is fleeting and surely not eternal.

I know of a young lady who has not made a commitment to accept Christ, yet she attends Bible studies and has even started to attend church with her Christian friends. *Why does she even go if she says she doesn't believe there is a God,* I thought. She's obtaining head knowledge and going through the motions for now, which is a good thing. What I love about this example is that her friends are not afraid to tell her the truth and challenge her way of thinking. They don't treat her any different because she doesn't think like they do. They don't get offended or make her feel condemned. They love her just as she is and are an excellent example of Christianity lived out. This is a beautiful illustration and reminder of evangelism/discipleship. Evangelism is twofold. There is the initial presentation of the plan of salvation but then there is the need to continue to teach and lead people. I do believe at some point it will go from her head to her heart, and when she does commit her life to Christ it will stick!

Jesus spent more time warning his listeners of the impending judgment of Hell than of the joys of Heaven. He was not afraid to speak truth! It was the mission from heaven to Jesus, as it is ours. We need to be willing to say to our family and friends, "I love you too much not to tell you the truth," or "I could never forgive myself if something happened to you and I never told you the truth about the gospel message. May I share it with you now?" If you are motivated by love, they will feel it. I can't say it enough, we have to speak truth in love even when it hurts or causes an initial negative reaction. Remember we are only the messengers. You only want to warn them and give them something to consider. When they are lying in their beds at night, they will remember the words you told them. At some point they will be faced with the realization of their mortality and where they may spend eternity. So when that day comes when our loved one's eyes are opened they will thank us for caring enough to not give up on them. Remember, the word of God never returns void and it will fulfill what it was sent out to accomplish in due season, so don't lose heart (see Isaiah 55:11).

But what if you have shared with them and they have not responded positively, this is when it can get tricky. The devil will try to create a wedge, but guard your relationship. Don't alienate them, let them know that your love is unconditional just like Jesus Christ's love. Be an excellent witness and pray for them often. I had a situation in my family where a person has chosen to alienate themselves because we do not agree with their lifestyle. We did not try to push them away nor tell them all the things they should change or stop doing. But because of our position and the conviction they feel, they are convinced we are against them which is not true. We told them we still love you and desire to have a relationship but that we can't condone their lifestyle.

I reminded them that our greatest concern is for their salvation. I said we are both sinners in need of a Savior. By accepting Jesus Christ as my Lord and Savior I now have a way to be forgiven and cleansed from my sin. Keep the main thing the main thing don't get caught up in passing judgement and pointing fingers. Deep down their conscience tells them it's wrong but they choose not to listen, so it separates them from God. That condemnation then keeps them out of church and distant from God's people and that means *you*! I know its hard but try and not take it personal. People try to avoid the truth until the truth becomes too big to overlook.

We all have had that breaking point and when that time comes, you will be there to welcome them back into the family. Just like the prodigal son who returned home after spending all his father's inheritance and when the father saw him coming home, he threw him a big party. (See Luke 15:11-32) The father did not chase after the son he let him go and believed God would one day restore their relationship. This is what we have to do sometimes, let them go for a time. Do not compromise your standard according to God's word for the relationship sake. Jesus said *we must hate our life and relationships in comparison to our love for God, Luke 14:26 (PARA)*. It's hard when you may have a wayward family member but just keep praying and believe that one day their eyes will be opened. The world says to be tolerant of everything and everybody, and when you don't tolerate sin they call us judgmental. Don't give into the pressure, stand for truth as much as it may hurt. Truth always prevails! Allow God to be your vindicator and to make all things right in his timing. Even when it looks like all hope is lost and there is no change, rest in knowing Holy Spirit is still working behind the scenes!

Be gentle and aware of the time and place and how you address your friends and family. Don't ever let it get into an argument. It's not a matter of who is right or wrong, but you are only warning them and sharing what you know to be true. Don't try to win the battle but lose the war. Remember their eyes are blinded for a time and they are deceived. We can't pressure or coerce people to make a commitment. We have to trust God's timing and believe their conscience will bear truth as they get a revelation for themselves of the love of God, the sacrifice He made for them and why.

Another witnessing conversation with a friend or family member may go like this:

"Please forgive me for not taking the time to ask you what you believe about God and where you think you will spend eternity when you die. Have you made peace with God? Have you ever prayed to receive Jesus Christ as your Savior? I was wondering if we could have a conversation about that now?" (always ask permission before you start). Let them talk and when they are finished you could share your testimony and then go into the gospel presentation. If their answer is no they have never prayed to receive Jesus. "Tell them there is a verse in the Bible that talks about how we all will be judged one day and have to give an account of our lives. *2 Corinthians 5:10 (NIV) says for we must all appear before the judgment seat of Christ, so that each of us may receive what is due us for the things done while in the body, whether good or bad.* "Can you imagine standing before the God of the Universe? I have given it serious thought.

The Bible also says, our goodness is like filthy rags and get us no access to heaven because we can't be good enough." *2 Thessalonians 1:8-9 (NIV) says: He will punish those who do not know God and do not obey the gospel of our Lord Jesus. They will be punished with everlasting destruction and shut out from the presence of the Lord.* "Jesus came to save us from spending eternity separated from God. *John 3:16 (NLT) For this is how God loved the world: He gave his one and only Son, so that everyone who believes in him will not perish but have eternal life.*" I don't want to spend eternity in hell separated from God and I'm sure you don't either. Jesus said, *I am the way the truth and the life no man goes to the Father except through Me. John 14:6 (PARA).*

"Having made Jesus my Lord and Savior was the best decision I ever made. What about you, what will you say when God asks you why should I let you into my heaven? The Bible also says we are saved by grace, that it's a free gift that God offers all of us. The gospel is simply believing Jesus is the son of God, that he died, rose from the grave and by the shedding of his blood on that cross we can be forgiven and cleansed from our sins. Through our repentance and trusting in this truth we can spend eternity in heaven because our righteousness is in him and not of ourselves. Does that make sense to you? Would you like to pray to receive Jesus Christ now?"

They may engage you further or shut it down, either way you've got them thinking. This conversation may go in lots of different directions but try and include the main points and memorize these key scriptures. Then let their conscience and the Holy Spirit do its work. You have done your part by planting a seed of truth and got them thinking about their eternity. You may want to have this book or your Bible with you so you can show them the scriptures to validate what you're telling them. Remember many people have never read the Bible and have no idea what it says. The Word of God is your most effective tool! That is why I have included so many scriptures in this book.

If someone you witness to wants to place their trust in Christ, there are several important things to emphasize they do right away so the devil doesn't snatch up the seed (Word of God) that was planted.

- Have them pray the prayer of salvation as you guide them along. *Romans 10:9 (NIV) If you declare with your mouth, "Jesus is LORD," and believe in your heart that God raised him from the dead, you will be saved.*
- It's essential that they get plugged into a local church and they be discipled. Be a mentor for them and hold them accountable. Invite them to your church or make a couple recommendations. Invite them to join you for Christian events, get-togethers at your house, they need to develop new Christian friends.
- Encourage them to be baptized. *Acts 2:38 (NASB) And Peter said to them, "Repent and be baptized every one of you in the name of Jesus Christ for the forgiveness of your sins, and you will receive the gift of the Holy Spirit.*
- Make sure they get a Bible. Use an easy to read translation, NIV or NLT are some good translations.
- Tell them to share with someone close to them as a testimony of what God has done. If they are ashamed to do that, they will not take a stand when it matters most. *Matthew 10:32-33 (NIV) "Therefore everyone who confesses Me before men, I will also confess him before My Father who is in heaven. But*

*whoever denies Me before men, I will also
deny him before My Father who is in heaven."*

ACTION ITEMS:

Start praying for the friend and/or family member you want to approach. Set up a time to talk, share your heart with them and your concern for their eternal salvation and where they will spend it.

[9]
ALLOW GOD OUT OF THE SUNDAY MORNING BOX

We need to incorporate our Christian life into our secular life and be willing to come out of our *Holy Huddles a*nd interact with unbelievers. Unfortunately, Christianity can become a subculture that isolates themselves from unbelievers. I believe we can maintain our boundaries of a holy lifestyle so we do not become like the world and yet still be in it.

Now I will say for the new believers who are trying to make a break from a former way of life, separating from that lifestyle may be necessary until you are mature and stable enough. God may give you opportunities at some point to witness to them, because the change in you will be a testament to the power of God and how it can change someone's life.

I believe there has been a misinterpretation of the

verse, *2 Corinthians 6:17 (NIV)* that says, *to come out from among them and touch no unclean thing.* We can take this too far and get to the point of thinking we are now better than unbelievers and not interact with them at all. The Apostle Paul says, *to be all things to all people.* He's not saying to compromise your standards and beliefs but rather to *be relatable*. I get it, we feel more comfortable around our Christian friends. It's easier and we tend to go with what's easy. But we are called to be *salt and light!*

Matthew 5:13-16 (NIV) You are the salt of the earth. But if the salt loses its saltiness, how can it be made salty again? It is no longer good for anything, except to be thrown out and trampled underfoot. You are the light of the world. A town built on a hill cannot be hidden. Neither do people light a lamp and put it under a bowl. Instead they put it on its stand, and it gives light to everyone in the house. In the same way, let your light shine before others, that they may see your good deeds and glorify your Father in heaven.

We don't have to be in full-time ministry to be "marketplace ministers". Our mission field may be our workplace, our neighborhood, our children's school or sports team, being a volunteer at our local hospital or nursing home. There are endless mission fields we can choose. We must allow God out of the *Sunday morning box* and allow Him to invade our lives. There are many people that may never walk through the doors of a church so we must be willing to go to them. That may require going to places that you never go. Has Father put on your heart a people group or place you have been afraid to reach? Do not fear because you may be the answer to someone's prayer for help!

The marketplace is our best and most easily reached mission field where we can be salt and light. You don't have to spend a dime to go there. When was the last time you looked at your job as a mission field and your ministry? We may pray *use me God* and He is saying, *I'm trying, look around you, the fields are ripe for the harvest, do you not see how depressed your coworker looks?* We need to change our mindset and look at our jobs as places the Lord has positioned us to be a witness. Take advantage of the divine appointments all around you. Start with an act of kindness, ask them how they are doing and then communicate how much Jesus knows and loves them. Offer to pray for them when and where appropriate.

Take the extra step to be kind to your co-worker or boss. I know this is not always easy. Our job can present lots of pressures to get things done quickly and people can really rub us the wrong way. But we need to be the best worker or boss, going above and beyond, be early, stay late, have the utmost integrity, being careful not to taint your witness. *Ephesians 4:1 (NLT) Therefore I, the prisoner of the Lord, implore you to walk in a manner worthy of the calling with which you have been called.* If we do lose our witness and say or do something contrary to how God calls us to conduct ourselves, confess your weaknesses AND APOLOGIZE! There is no bigger turn off to unbelievers than a self righteous person. They will appreciate your humility and transparency.

I have been a financial advisor for 30 years and I help people plan for the future. There have been many times where I have prayed with people in my office or over the phone. It catches them off guard at first because they don't expect it in a work environment. But , I have never had anyone refuse prayer. There was this one man, I wasn't sure if he was a Christian or not, but I asked if I could pray for him over the phone because he had lost his wife. He later told me it was the nicest thing anyone has ever done for him! I didn't think much of it, just a little prayer, but to him it was huge. He even asked me if he could play my CD at his wife's funeral and so many got to hear the gospel message!

We just never know what may come out of an opportunity. I do know that whenever we are obedient to the Lord's still small voice it always brings fruit. I even went a step further and sent a CD to every one of my clients for their birthday. The response has been overwhelming. They call and thank me, and many have asked if they could buy some for their friends and family. I don't worry if they are believers or not, I just treat them all the same.

When we do this we are showing people we are not too busy to notice them. I like to affirm people by telling them that God knows them, loves them and believes in them.

Living on mission is a way of life, we're on 24/7, it's not a program or an event, says Todd White of Lifestyle Christianity. Todd White's ministry started by praying for people in the streets. After he prayed for over 400 people, he finally started to see miracle after miracle healings. I love to watch his videos of being out on the streets praying and healing people. Make a point to watch them, they will build your faith and encourage you to believe that you too can pray for the sick and they will recover. *James 5:15 (NIV) And the prayer offered in faith will make the sick person well; the Lord will raise them up. If they have sinned, they will be forgiven.*

I have personally prayed for people and seen immediate healings here and abroad. I know for a fact that God heals and when someone experiences this type of supernatural event they can't deny there is a God. This is another one of the tools available to you as a believer. It is one of the spiritual gifts the Bible says God empowers to everyone who asks and believes. *Mark 16:20 (AMP) And they went out and preached everywhere, while the Lord kept working with them and confirming the message by the attesting signs and miracles that closely accompanied [it]. Amen (so be it).*

The preaching of the gospel and miracles go hand in

hand. But remember, whether you see an immediate result or not that shouldn't stop us from praying for people! I prayed for a woman in my exercise class just the other day. I didn't know if she believed in God or healing but it didn't matter because God said to pray. Well she didn't experience anything different at that moment but 2 days later I saw her again and the shooting pain was gone. Praise God! It's not all about the outcome but the act of obedience apart from the outcome Every obedient act is a way to shape and mold us into the image of Christ.

We are ambassadors of the gospel everywhere we go. *2 Cor.5:20 (NIV) we are therefore Christ's ambassadors, as though God were making his appeal through us. We implore you on Christ's behalf: Be reconciled to God.* An ambassador is a representation of the kingdom. They represent and speak on behalf of that kingdom. Sharing your faith is not just something we do, it's who we are as children of an eternal kingdom. I truly believe we are beginning to see God raising up a mighty army of evangelists that are not on the platforms but in the streets. It's people like you and me!

Deut. 6:4-5 (NIV) "Hear, O Israel: The Lord our God, the Lord is one. You shall love the Lord your God with all your heart and with all your soul and with all your might. And these words that I command you today shall be on your heart. You shall teach them diligently to your children and shall talk of them when you sit in your house, and when you walk by the way, and when you lie down, and when you rise. You shall bind them as a sign on your hand, and they shall be as frontlets between your eyes. You shall write them on the doorposts of your house and on your gates.

This scripture reminds us to *be intentional as we go about our daily life*. If we don't keep a kingdom mindset and our desire to please the Lord on the forefront of our brains we will go about our day and never give it another thought. We are such selfish creatures and it's always about SELF. This is probably our biggest challenge because we are always busy doing our own thing or completing our *To Do* list. Now I will admit, I fall short and when I'm too busy to stop and notice or speak to someone. I get frustrated with myself and vow to do better the next time.

I don't want God to choose someone else to do it and "miss out on my blessing", as they say in the South. We need to ask the Holy Spirit to help us be more aware of the opportunities around us and to look at ourselves as the "watchman on the wall." Pray every morning before you start your day that your eyes will be open to the divine appointments. *2 Chronicles 16:9 (NLT) says, the eyes of the LORD search the whole earth in order to strengthen those whose hearts are fully committed to him.* People are more open to conversations about spiritual matters than most realize. Everyone is searching for the truth. It's just a matter of *whose truth* they will believe.

We are the counterbalance to the world and all other religions.

So, once we're in a position to share with someone how do we open that spiritual conversation? First, we must know our audience and the way to do that is by asking questions and being interested in what they have to say. It's more about listening at this point than you presenting the gospel. We must know their view of God before we know how to present the gospel.

Evangelism Explosion uses a questionnaire method which is a good way to open a spiritual conversation with people we know or with strangers. If you do this with strangers it is best to go two by two, any more than that and it can be intimidating for people you approach. Young people really seem to like answering questionnaires because they want to be heard. Remember most people's favorite subject is themselves. Why do you think so many people take selfies! When I approach someone, *I introduce myself and tell them, "We are from the local church, youth group, etc. and we are asking people questions to see how they would answer. Would you have any objections to answering a few questions and giving us your perspective relating to spiritual matters?"* These are some of the questions I use. You may want to create your own list.

- What is your religious background?

- Do you believe there is only one Sovereign God?
- What do you think happens when people die?
- Do you believe in heaven and hell?
- You never know when you're going to die, but suppose you died today and you were standing in the presence of Almighty God, and God asked you. Why should I allow you to enter Heaven for eternity? What reason would you give to God?
- Do you know how you can be forgiven of your sins?
- Do you believe Jesus was the Son of God?

The answer to these questions will help you to know where to go next with the conversation. If they have a misguided theology try to specifically address that and see what has brought them to that conclusion then present the gospel of Jesus Christ. The more you do this the better you will get with your responses and knowing where to take the conversation. It's like anything, you have to practice to get better. The most reassuring thing is knowing that you have the Holy Spirit to guide you and bring to remembrance the Word of God. Trust what you have learned and instilled in your heart and what is in you will flow out of you. It does take a step of faith but as many times I have done it Holy Spirit has never failed me yet!

Another way to open the door with someone is random acts of kindness. I love this one because the act itself will open the heart to better receive from you. Pay for someone's meal, groceries, coffee, leave a ridiculously good tip, watch their kids for free, give up your seat in a crowded place, visit someone in a nursing home, a friendly hello, to mention a few ideas. Get creative and intentional and be amazed how receptive people will be. One time my family and I were out blessing people with money. I approached this woman in a Walmart with $100.00. She immediately started to cry because she had just given her last $100.00 to someone she felt needed it worse than she did. She wrestled with doing it because she didn't have much herself, but she obeyed God and He immediately replaced it with my gift. How cool is God?

But remember, words must follow the deed. Many are willing to do a good deed but then not follow up with the Good News and prayer. We are doing people a disservice if we meet a physical need and do not address their spiritual needs. We must do both! If we only give them water they will be thirsty again the next day but if we give them living water they will never thirst again. Isn't that what Jesus told the woman at the well. So why do we fall short when it comes to praying and sharing the gospel with people? I believe there are lots of reasons as we talked about in previous chapters but primarily I think we make it more about ourselves and we are not fully trusting God. We must be motivated by our love for God! Out of a heart of thanksgiving we give back to him in the ways we minister to others. Matthew 25:40 (NIV), "The King will reply, 'Truly I tell you, whatever you did for one of the least of these brothers and sisters of mine, you did for me.'"

You can say a lot in a prayer, and hardly anyone ever says no when asked if they would like prayer. Most people are so thankful and surprised by that act of kindness. It seems so simple yet many people only give others lip service by saying they'll pray for them. It is not the same as that personal touch of praying right then. Use your prophetic gift to discern a sickness or pain and pray for their healing. Give them a word of knowledge. Pray a blessing over them and ask if there is something specific you can pray for. By praying for people you show concern, love, and you allow the power of God to flow through you by the laying on of hands. *Luke 4:40 says Jesus laid His hands on each one of sick and afflicted as He was healing them and also in Acts 1:18 we see the disciples laid hands on the people and they received the Holy Spirit.*

We need to believe for the supernatural fire and power of God to fall on people when we pray. I believe we will see a rise in this supernatural move of God as we continue to yield to his agenda and not ours. As we obey the leading of the Spirit in the *Who, What, When and Where* he will show up because he wants to demonstrate how much he loves his children. People may not believe what you say but one touch from God can radically change a person's heart!

If you don't have a lot of time to talk, have witnessing tools you can leave with them. That is the reason I produced my CD called *The Simple Gospel*. I give my CD's away everywhere I go. It is so easy and people are always very appreciative. As they listen to the CD, it takes them on a journey of realizing who Jesus is, why He came, the plan of salvation and what our purpose is on this earth. This unique presentation of the gospel though worship and the spoken word is a way to plant a seed that they can listen to over and over and even pass on to someone else. I found that worship music opens the heart to better receive the word of God. Even though I produced it for the person who doesn't know Jesus Christ, believers have found it very encouraging as well.

You can also use Gospel Tracts, two of my favorites are *Eternal Life* by the North American Mission Board or *Do you know?* When using tracts just make sure they are balanced. I have found too many preach the "happiness gospel" and not the full gospel which has the balance of law and grace. I also like to give away the *Book of John* booklet, *The Case for Christ* by Lee Strobel (great for the atheists), or the New Testament Bible.

ACTION ITEMS:

Engage someone in a spiritual conversation using one of the tools. Invite your unsaved neighbor or co-worker to your home for dinner and be intentional about rubbing elbows with non-believers.

[10]
BUILD A BRIDGE

I WANT TO DEDICATE A CHAPTER OF THIS BOOK TO witnessing to Muslims because they are becoming the most prominent religion compared to Christianity. Islam is the fastest growing religion in the world today, nearly 1 out of every 5 people is a Muslim. Did you know that 6 out of every 7 Muslims are not Arab. They are very moral people and adhere to very strict law called Sharia Law.

According to Scholastic Update, Islam is the fastest growing religion in the United States. One of the reasons is the high birth rate. Of the eleven hundred mosques in America, 80% have been built in the last 12 years. Since 1900, the Muslim religion has doubled every 24 years. From 1944 to 1979 the number doubled from 400 million to 800 million. It doubled again in 2003 to around 1.6 billion.

Sadly, Christianity only doubles, on average, every 47

years based on this same study. The Muslim people do revere and love the Jesus Christ of the Quran. They believe that they honor Him more than Christians because they do not believe that God would have subjected Him to the humiliation and pain of crucifixion. Muslims reject the Trinity—that God has revealed Himself as one in three Persons: the Father, Son, and Holy Spirit. They don't believe he was the son of God but that he was an apostle/prophet of God.

However, even the Quran addresses the fact that Jesus prophesied His death and resurrection. In fact, many of the references in the Quran speak of Him as being the Word, the Messiah, the one nearest to God, and the Spirit of God. Many Muslim people honor Jesus, yet their minds and hearts have been blinded from the truth of His mission.

The History of Islam:

In the seventh century, Muhammad claimed the angel Gabriel visited him. During these angelic visitations, which continued for about 23 years until Muhammad's death, the angel purportedly revealed to Muhammad the words of Allah. These dictated revelations compose the Qur'an, Islam's holy book.

Some Definitions:

- Allah: The word for God in Arabic.
- Arab: A person whose native tongue is Arabic or who identifies with other Arabs of an ethnic group. Arab is defined independent of religious identity.
- Islam: Submission to God, or total commitment to the authority and power of God. It is the faith, submission, and practice of the Muslim people.
- Jihad: Struggle or effort in the path of God. It can be used to describe a personal internal struggle, but it is usually used to describe a defensive "Just War" to protect or spread Islam. They call it "Holy War."
- Muslim: One who is submitted to God, one whose religion is Islam.
- Quran: Recitation in Arabic; they believe that this book contains a message from God recited by Muhammad and recorded by his followers.

The Doctrine of Islam:

Muslims summarize their doctrine in six articles of faith:

1. Belief in one Allah: Muslims believe Allah is one, eternal, creator, and sovereign.
2. Belief in the angels
3. Belief in the prophets: The prophets include the biblical prophets but end with Muhammad as Allah's final prophet.
4. Belief in the revelations of Allah: Muslims accept certain portions of the Bible, such as the Torah and the Gospels. They believe the Qur'an is the preexistent, perfect word of Allah.
5. Belief in the last day of judgment and the hereafter: Everyone will be resurrected for judgment into either paradise or hell.
6. Belief in predestination: Muslims believe Allah has decreed everything that will happen. Muslims testify to Allah's sovereignty with their frequent phrase, *inshallah*, meaning, "if God wills."

The Five Pillars of Islam:

These five tenets compose the framework of obedience for Muslims:

1. The testimony of faith (*shahada*): "*la ilaha illa allah. Muhammad rasul Allah.*" This means, "There is no deity but Allah.

Muhammad is the messenger of Allah." A person can convert to Islam by stating this creed. The shahada shows that a Muslim believes in Allah alone as deity and believes that Muhammad reveals Allah.

2. Prayer (*salat*): Five ritual prayers must be performed every day.
3. Giving (*zakat*): This almsgiving is a certain percentage given once a year.
4. Fasting (*sawm*): Muslims fast during Ramadan in the ninth month of the Islamic calendar. They must not eat or drink from dawn until sunset.
5. Pilgrimage (*hajj*): If physically and financially possible, a Muslim must make the pilgrimage to Mecca in Saudi Arabia at least once. The *hajj* is performed in the twelfth month of the Islamic calendar.

A Muslim's entrance into paradise hinges on obedience to these Five Pillars. Still, Allah may reject them. Even Muhammad was not sure whether Allah would admit him to paradise (Surah 46:9; Hadith 5.266).

We need to build a bridge not put up walls to reach them. The bridge we need to apply in order to connect with the Muslim faith is the mighty name of Jesus Christ. The approach to take in witnessing to Muslims is very similar to the approach Jesus took with His disciples in Matthew 16:13-18. He first asks them, "Who do men say that I the Son of man am?" He then asks them "Who do you say that I am?" Our question to the Muslim people is, "Who does the Quran say that Jesus Christ is? And who do you say that Jesus Christ is?"

Our approach should be to have friendly dialogue about who Jesus Christ is. We should discuss Jesus from the Quran perspective as well as the biblical perspective without shutting them down. This focuses the conversation on Jesus and allows the individual to really question their true beliefs and perspectives. This will also allow the Holy Spirit to start working. The challenge for us is in trusting that the Holy Spirit will remove the blindness as we begin to speak about the things that we may readily agree upon.

Most Muslims will agree with the statement that Jesus is the Messiah, as well as the Word of God. However, they are left with the conclusion that He was just a prophet. As we discussed earlier, it is our goal to apply Matthew 16:13-18.

We must first have a basic understanding of what the Quran has to say about Jesus Christ. Then, find out what the person that we are communicating with has to say about Jesus. The goal of this method is to keep the conversation to the name of Jesus, discussing its use in the Quran, while showing them what the Holy Bible has to say.

Rather than getting defensive or trying to disprove

Islam, try to direct the conversation to what is important, the person of Jesus Christ! Keep in mind that it is our goal to create bridges, not destroy them. By attempting to attack Muhammad, or Allah, or any other religion the unbeliever's distaste for Christians only grows, creating walls and barriers. We trust that the Holy Spirit will do the real work and change their hearts as we simply speak of the Jesus Christ that is found in the Bible!

Begin by Asking Them:

1. Isn't it true that the Quran says that Jesus Christ is the Word of God?

Quran References: Surah 4:171 "People of the Book, do not transgress the bounds of your religion. Speak nothing but the truth about God. The Messiah, Jesus the son of Mary, no more than God's apostle and His Word which He cast to Mary."

2. Isn't it true that the Quran affirms that Jesus was born of a virgin birth?

Quran References: Surah 3:47 "Lord,' she said, 'how can I bear a child when no man has touched me?' 'Even thus God creates whom He will." Surah 19:20 "How shall I bear a child,' she answered, 'when I have neither been touched by any man nor ever been unchaste?"

3. Isn't it true that the Quran says that Jesus is the Messiah?

Quran References: Surah 3:45 "His name is the Messiah." Surah 5:75 "The Messiah, the son of Mary."

4. Doesn't the Quran indicate that Jesus was sinless?

Quran References: Surah 19:30 "He has exhorted me to honor my mother and has purged me of vanity and wickedness."

5. Doesn't the Quran say that Jesus prophesied His death and His Resurrection?

Quran References: Surah 3:56 "God said: 'Jesus, I am about to claim you back and lift you up to Me. I shall take you away from the unbelievers and exalt your followers above them until the Day of Resurrection." Surah 19:34 "Blessed was I on the day I was born, and blessed I shall be on the day of my death and on the day, I shall be raised to life."

6. Doesn't the Quran indicate that Jesus is the Spirit of God?

Quran References: Surah 4:171 "Christ Jesus the Son of Mary was an apostle of God, and His Word, which He bestowed on Mary, and a Spirit proceeding from Him." Surah 2:87 "We gave Jesus the son of Mary clear (signs) and strengthened him with the Holy Spirit

In conclusion, once you have discussed the similarities and differences, then share the good news, and the true mission of Jesus Christ. Explain that their sin has separated them from God and that the only way to inherit eternal life is by accepting the free gift of salvation through Jesus Christ. It is not of their works. *Jesus is the way, the truth and the life and no man goes to the Father except through him John 14:6.* Share the Good News and what the true mission of Christ was. Ask them if they want to pray to receive Jesus as their Savior. Remember we only distance ourselves further from those that are lost when we attack their religion or become defensive.

And lastly, we do not need to fear them nor see them as the enemy. Although I do realize that if you are in a Muslim country that forbids the preaching of the gospel you must be very careful and adhere to the guidelines set forth by the missionary organizations. We can't be a loose cannon and put yourself and others lives in jeopardy. Also people that convert to Christianity can be excommunicated or even put to death. We must be sensitive to their plight. Above all we remember they are a child of God and he desires that they too come to the saving knowledge of the truth of the gospel message.

[11]
OH NO, YOU DIDN'T, OH YES, I DID!

THE DON'TS:

Don't have a holier than thou attitude, don't be judgmental, don't try to win the argument and lose the convert, it is not a debate. Don't talk too much, don't talk too loud, don't be flakey or super-spiritual, don't get in their face, don't be too touchy, don't be too preachy, don't use religious terminology "Christianese", don't criticize or attack, don't assume they know who Jesus is and why He came, don't condemn and get defensive. It's not about proving who's right and who's wrong.

I'd like to share with you two witnessing styles. I like to witness to people on our beaches. It's a great place to approach people because they are not in a hurry and they are usually happy to talk. One day I approached a young man and asked if I could ask him a few questions relating to spiritual matters. He said *sure*, I told him I didn't feel it was by chance that we were talking about God because it seemed as if God went out of his way to bring him to Florida on this specific day to be approached by me.

We had a very engaging conversation and I left him a book called *More than a Carpenter* by Josh McDowell, which I highly recommend as a witnessing tool to leave with analytical people. I told him that nothing is by chance and I believed Jesus was offering him the chance to accept Him and have eternal life. I prayed for him, he thanked me and off I went. He was not offended, and seeds were planted. He didn't pray to receive Christ right then, but it was still a successful witnessing opportunity.

The other example starts off the same with a questionnaire but this time my friend overtakes the conversation, she doesn't take time to listen. The conversation is filled with her quoting scripture and basically preaching a message. The young people are overwhelmed, out of the four she is speaking to, two are saved, two are not sure. They were pressured to recite the sinner's prayer and she told them she would baptize them right then in the Gulf of Mexico. The one girl looked at me as if to say *help me* and said, "I just washed my hair." I told them *it's okay you don't have to do it now, but when you get plugged into a church, seek to be baptized at one of their baptism services.*

So, which one do you think was the right way? You may be thinking, well in the second example the young people said the sinner's prayer. But remember we are not saved by just reciting a prayer. Father is looking for disciples not decisions makers. It's a heart of repentance, with a cry in their heart that is a sign of a true convert. I cannot emphasize enough that just because someone didn't say the sinner's prayer right then doesn't mean you failed or what you said didn't matter. The word never returns void!

Isaiah 55:10 (NIV) As the rain and the snow come down from heaven, and do not return to it without watering the earth and making it bud and flourish, so that it yields seed for the sower and bread for the eater, so is my word that goes out from my mouth: It will not return to me empty, but will accomplish what I desire and achieve the purpose for which I sent it. It will perform what it was sent out to do in due season.

I am not here to judge either way but I share these two scenarios to emphasize the importance of being sensitive and not making people feel coerced. This is also why I'm not in favor of only using one methodology. If we get too hung up on following a script, we could miss the leading of the Spirit in pursuit of our agenda. You may never approach a stranger on a beach, but be ready whenever the Lord offers you a divine appointment. Be yourself, be sincere and speak truth in love!

It is more important to ask the right questions, as opposed to having all the right answers. If we don't ask the questions how will we know where they stand? Quite often Jesus answered a question with a question. Put the burden of proof on them. Make them prove to you why they believe what they believe. Ask them where they get their information and how trustworthy is it. Sometimes by them just verbalizing what they believe they start to realize how flawed their belief may be. You want to skillfully dismantle their false belief system and asking questions is the best way to do this. If we can remove the walls that support the roof, the house of their belief system will fall. It's okay if you don't have all the answers. Some things we just can't explain because we believe them by faith. *Hebrews 11:1 (ESV) now faith is the assurance of things hoped for, the conviction of things not seen.*

Jesus said, *blessed is the man who hasn't seen and still believes.* Don't be intimidated or afraid of a little friction. Almost expect it, so if you don't get *push back* you'll be pleasantly surprised! Don't feel bad if someone wants to end a conversation or gets defensive, it means they are feeling conviction and that's a good thing! It means their conscience is bearing with the truth.

1 Peter 3:13-17 (ESV) now who is there to harm you if you are zealous for what is good? But even if you should suffer for righteousness sake, you will be blessed. Have no fear of them, nor be troubled, but in your hearts honor Christ the Lord as holy, always being prepared to make a defense to anyone who asks you for a reason for the hope that is in you; yet do it with gentleness and respect, having a good conscience, so that, when you are slandered, those who revile your good behavior in Christ may be put to shame. For it is better to suffer for doing good, if that should be God's will, than for doing evil.

It's more important to fear God and live to please Him than to be a people pleaser and appease people. Everybody loses when we live like that. It's a trap and the devil's tool to shut us up and keep us intimidated. Let the Holy Spirit do His work as you sow the seeds of God's love and Word.

THE DO'S:

Be friendly and kind, be considerate, maintain eye contact and don't wear sunglasses, let them see the love through your eyes, ask permission to speak to them, show genuine love and compassion, ask lots of questions, have your ministering equipment; i.e. Tracts, Bibles, list of questions, money, something to leave with them. Build a bridge not a wall. Earn the right to be heard. Be a person of honor and integrity, be respectful and an excellent witness, keep your life pure and holy, don't give a brother a reason to stumble.

Always keep in mind that *salvation* is the issue and not their present sufferings or sin. We can really get sidetracked and create a more defensive position in the listener if we attack their lifestyle and start telling them all the things they need to stop doing. Instead focus on their relationship with Jesus. He'll clean them up once they surrender to Him.

I heard this great analogy from Ray Comfort about *keeping the main thing the main thing*. There was a little boy running through the woods who fell and a tree branch plunged into his jugular vein area. As his father rushed to his rescue, he applied pressure to the wound and took his son to the emergency room. As the physician examined the boy, the boy cried out, "doctor, doctor I hurt," the doctor said, "I know your neck is wounded." "No, no" said the little boy "I have a splinter in my finger, take it out now!" The doctor, of course, told the boy he would get to that once the bleeding was stopped. The bleeding that could cost him his life. This is what happens when people want us to focus on problems and issues. They can sidetrack us from addressing the most important issue, which is the person's eternal salvation.

It is important to let people know we care about their troubles but we don't have the answers to all their problems, however, God's word does have the answers. We should try to help meet their physical needs, but if we stop there and let them walk away, not giving them an opportunity to accept Jesus Christ and apply the life saving measures that will ultimately save their lives for eternity, we are doing them a disservice. They may not have another opportunity to hear and receive salvation.

I led a medical missions trip to Honduras recently and as we set up our stations for the day. We made sure to have a prayer station where we could pray for their healing. We told them *we can give you medicine but God is the Great Physician and it is He who heals and saves.* We saw many healings that day and we praised God for His faithfulness to allow us to see signs and wonders accompany the preaching of the gospel. It was a beautiful example of meeting a physical and spiritual need in one outreach. As you plan your outreaches make sure to keep this balance and offer both. Don't assume they will understand the *why* behind what you are doing. There are good people doing great things but just being nice doesn't win people over to the truth and the saving knowledge of the gospel. The devil will counterfeit good deeds and the supernatural to deceive people. So unless people say in whose name they are doing these things, it could be a counterfeit.

Share your testimony. *Revelation 12:11 (NASB) reads: "And they overcame him because of the blood of the Lamb and because of the word of their testimony, and they did not love their lives even when faced with death."* Our testimony is a powerful evangelism tool we have at our disposal. Because it's our life, and no one can contest what Jesus has done in us. Just remember to keep it short. You don't have to preach a message. Just be yourself. Make sure the *after Christ days* are emphasized more than the *before Christ days.* Some people can really glorify their past sins. Write it out and practice it so you don't ramble on and on. I don't agree with the quote that says, "live out the gospel and when necessary use words." We must use words!

Romans 10:14 (NLT) But how can they call on him to save them unless they believe in him? And how can they believe in him if they have never heard about him? And how can they hear about him unless someone tells them? And how will anyone go and tell them without being sent? That is why the Scriptures say, 'How beautiful are the feet of messengers who bring good news!' The primary way God works is through people and the verbalization of the gospel. It will not just happen through osmosis!

I've been in some type of sales my entire career and we are taught to have an *elevator speech* so that when the opportunity presents itself, we can tell people what we do and why. It should be short and powerful enough to catch their attention. It's the same with presenting the gospel. We need to be impactful and compelling in how we explain the hope we have and why someone else would want it. The Bible says to be ready, do the work to show yourself approved in 2 *Tim. 4:2-5 (NIV) preach the Word; be ready in season and out of season; reprove, rebuke, and exhort, with complete patience and teaching. For the time is coming when people will not endure sound teaching but having itching ears, they will accumulate for themselves teachers to suit their own passions and will turn away from listening to the truth and wander off into myths. As for you, always be sober- minded, endure suffering, do the work of an evangelist, fulfill your ministry.*

You don't have to be the pushy salesman. Just present the gospel in a loving and simple way. The decision is up to them. Don't get discouraged and focus on the *no's* but always looking for the *yes*. Remember every *no* could be just a delayed yes! Unfortunately, all are invited but few come. *Matt: 7:13-14 (NIV) Enter through the narrow gate. For wide is the gate and broad is the road that leads to destruction, and many enter through it. But small is the gate and narrow the road that leads to life, and only a few find it.*

ACTION ITEMS:

Compile your testimony and practice it on a close friend or family member. Ask them for a constructive critique.

[12]
OVERCOMING THE TOP 10 OBJECTIONS

1. WHAT ABOUT THE PEOPLE WHO HAVE NEVER HEARD ABOUT JESUS WHO LIVE IN REMOTE PLACES? HOW CAN THEY GO TO HELL IF THEY HAVE NEVER HEARD?

A PERSON DOES NOT GO TO HELL BECAUSE HE HASN'T heard of Jesus but because he sinned against God. Sin is the transgression of the Law. God will make sure everyone is given the opportunity to accept or reject Him. Jesus is the solution not the cause! Because of the internet and the bible being translated into many languages more and more areas of the world are being evangelized. We are also assured in Scripture in *Revelation 7:9,* that God will be worshipped by *"a great multitude that no one could count, from every nation, tribe, people and language."* We are within range of penetrating every people group on the planet with the light of the gospel with more momentum than ever before in history. You could even say, "If you are concerned about these people, my friend, maybe God is calling you to go and be a part of declaring His glory to the nations!"

God is also seen in nature and in everything around us and is perceived within. *Romans 1:19 (NIV) For since the creation of the world God's invisible qualities—his eternal power and divine nature—have been clearly seen, being understood from what has been made, so that people are without excuse.* It is just an issue of whether or not He is acknowledged.

I have heard of stories where Jesus revealed Himself to people before they even knew who He was. There is a story in the Book of Martys where a man in a Muslim country experienced the presence of Jesus in his home and he was saved without anyone ever telling him about Christianity. God is a supernatural God and is beyond time and space and He can reveal himself any way He wants. *2 Peter (NIV) 3:9 says, The Lord is not slow in keeping his promise, as some understand slowness. Instead he is patient with you, not wanting anyone to perish, but everyone to come to repentance.*

2. WHY IS THERE SUFFERING? THAT PROVES THERE IS NO LOVING GOD.

We live in a fallen world and everything in it is in a constant state of death and decay. The Bible says in

Romans 5:12 (ESV) Therefore, just as sin came into the world through one man, and death through sin, and so death spread to all men because all sinned. Disease, suffering, and death entered the world as a result of the original sin. So, we shouldn't blame God, but rather *man*. Rather than viewing suffering an excuse to reject God, it should be the very reason to turn to God. It is a great mystery why God allows suffering, but despite the mystery, the Christian learns to trust God. What the devil means for evil and destruction God can use for good.

Romans 8:18-20 (NLT) Yet what we suffer now is nothing compared to the glory he will reveal to us later. For all creation is waiting eagerly for that future day when God will reveal who his children really are. Against its will, all creation was subjected to God's curse. The creation looks forward to the day when it will join God's children in glorious freedom from death and decay.

For we know that all creation has been groaning as in the pains of childbirth right up to the present time. And we believers also groan, even though we have the Holy Spirit within us as a foretaste of future glory, for we long for our bodies to be released from sin and suffering. We, too, wait with eager hope for the day when God will give us our full rights as his adopted children, including the new bodies he has promised us. Suffering may be the reality for a time but Father promises one day we will have no more pain or suffering when we get our new bodies!

We will never fully understand why innocent people

suffer but we do know that evil is a result of free will and that innocent people are hurt by our sin. The only way God could remove all suffering is to remove evil and to remove all evil means to remove our free will.

3. I BELIEVE IN EVOLUTION.

First we have to acknowledge that species have indeed changed over time to survive, but the theory of evolution mistakenly claims that those adaptations can actually result in the creation of new species. It also inaccurately claims that life itself could have randomly evolved from non-living material. The mathematical probability of life originating at random is miniscule. The earth's fossil record reveals that every living form has appeared suddenly and completely developed - not through gradual transition, as the evolution theory would suggest. It's irrational to believe that something can come from nothing, that chaos birthed order, and that lifeless matter produced consciousness.

Remember that, while evolutionists claim that biological life arose accidentally, people don't see information arising accidentally anywhere in the physical world. Accepting the theory of evolution requires faith, just as believing in creationism does, because no human alive today can travel back in time to observe what happened when the universe began. Creationism is just as scientific as evolution, because each seeks to explain within its framework all the real known data of science and history. While the Bible leaves the time frame of creation left to some interpretation, we are given a little insight in the verse, *2 Peter 3:8 (ESV) But do not overlook this one fact, beloved, that with the Lord one day is as a thousand years, and a thousand years as one day*, the point isn't how much time the process took. The Bible is very clear about what matters most—Who is responsible for creation (God).

Colossians 1:16 (NLT) For through him God created everything in the heavenly realms and on earth. He made the things we can see and the things we can't see— such as thrones, kingdoms, rulers, and authorities in the unseen world. Everything was created through him and for him. The bottom line is *being reconciled back to God and our salvation,* the rest can be debated and is only a distraction to the truth.

4. I DON'T BELIEVE IN GOD

The evidence of God is seen in His unique authority and power. While this evidence is more subjective, it is no less a powerful testimony of His divine presence. This authority and power are best seen in the way countless lives have been transformed by the supernatural power of God. The sick and afflicted have been healed, those in bondage to sin set free, hardened criminals reformed, and hate turned to love. The God of the universe does possess a dynamic and transforming supernatural power which is displayed in what we call *miracles*. You can't explain them, but the results are no less real.

We also see in *Romans 1:18-31 (NIV) The wrath of God is being revealed from heaven against all the godlessness and wickedness of people, who suppress the truth by their wickedness, since what may be known about God is plain to them, because God has made it plain to them. For since the creation of the world God's invisible qualities—his eternal power and divine nature—have been clearly seen, being understood from what has been made, so that people are without excuse. For although they knew God, they neither glorified him as God nor gave thanks to him, but their thinking became futile and their foolish hearts were darkened. Although they claimed to be wise, they became fools and exchanged the glory of the immortal God for images made to look like a mortal human being and birds and animals and reptiles.*

Therefore God gave them over in the sinful desires of their hearts to sexual impurity for the degrading of their bodies with one another. They exchanged the truth about God for a lie and worshiped and served created things rather than the Creator—who is forever praised. Amen. Because of this, God gave them over to shameful lusts. Even their women exchanged natural sexual relations for unnatural ones. In the same way the men also abandoned natural relations with women and were inflamed with lust for one another. Men committed shameful acts with other men and received in themselves the due penalty for their error. Furthermore, just as they did not think it worthwhile to retain the knowledge of God, so God gave them over to a depraved mind, so that they do what ought not to be done. They have become filled with every kind of wickedness, evil, greed and depravity.

They are full of envy, murder, strife, deceit and malice. They are gossips, slanderers, God-haters, insolent, arrogant and boastful; they invent ways of doing evil; they disobey their parents; they have no understanding, no fidelity, no love, no mercy. Although they know God's righteous decree that those who do such things deserve death, they not only continue to do these very things but also approve of those who practice them.

I thought it necessary to write out this entire chapter of Romans 1 because there is so much in it that we see today all around us. People know deep down there is a God but they choose not to see and recognize him so they can satisfy their sinful desires. The original sin was unbelief, not the fact Adam and Eve disobeyed God's command to not eat from the tree of knowledge. It started with unbelief in that what God said would truly happen, from there becomes a very slippery slope to depravity. Many people are convinced their way is right. *Proverbs 14:12 (NIV) There is a way that appears to be right, but in the end, it leads to death.* It's a huge chance to take!

Just because we don't see something doesn't make it not real. When you see a building, you must know that there was a builder by the evidence. Remember your job isn't to convince the person that there is a God according to Romans 1:20, his conscience already knows that. You are to have a conversation that challenges their way of thinking and plants a seed of doubt that their belief system could be flawed.

5. I DON'T BELIEVE THE BIBLE IS THE INSPIRED WORD OF GOD. IT WAS JUST WRITTEN BY MEN.

The Bible has hundreds of fulfilled prophecies and there is plenty of scientific evidence that confirms the Bible is the inspired Word of God. God authored the writing but used men to be the instrument. The Bible is the most published and read book in the world. Ask people if they have ever read it? Then simply challenge them to read it for themselves. How can they speak of something they have never explored or read? The Bible is God's instruction manual for life, and to protect us from evil. *2 Timothy (ESV) 3:16–17 Scripture is breathed out by God and profitable for teaching, for reproof, for correction, and for training in righteousness, that the man of God may be complete, equipped for every good work.*

There is both internal and external evidence that the Bible is truly God's Word. The internal evidence includes those things within the Bible that testify of its divine origin. The first internal evidence that the Bible is truly God's Word, is seen in its unity. Even though it is really sixty-six individual books, written on three continents, in three different languages, over a period of approximately 1,500 years, by more than 40 authors who came from many walks of life, the Bible remains one unified book from beginning to end without contradiction. This unity is unique from all other books and is evidence of the divine origin of the words which God moved men to record.

Another internal evidence that indicates the Bible is truly God's Word is the prophecies contained within its pages. The Bible contains hundreds of detailed prophecies relating to the future of individual nations, including Israel, certain cities, and mankind. There are over three hundred prophecies concerning Jesus Christ in the Old Testament. Not only was it foretold where He would be born and His lineage, but also how He would die and that He would rise again. There simply is no logical way to explain the fulfilled prophecies in the Bible other than by divine origin. There is no other religious book with the extent or type of predictive prophecy that the Bible contains.

Through both archaeological evidence and other writings, the historical accounts of the Bible have been proven time and time again to be accurate and true. In fact, all the archaeological and manuscript evidence supporting the Bible makes it the best-documented book from the ancient world. The fact that the Bible accurately and truthfully records historically verifiable events is a great indication of its truthfulness.

Another external evidence that the Bible is truly God's Word is the integrity of its human authors. As mentioned earlier, God used men from many walks of life to record His words. In studying the lives of these men, we find them to be honest and sincere. The fact that they were willing to die, often excruciating deaths, for what they believed testifies that these ordinary, yet honest men truly believed God had spoken to them. The men who wrote the New Testament and many hundreds of other believers (1 Corinthians 15:6) knew the truth of their message because they had seen and spent time with Jesus Christ after He had risen from the dead. Seeing the risen Christ had a tremendous impact on them. They went from hiding in fear, to being willing to die for the message God had revealed to them. Their lives and deaths testify to the fact that the Bible truly is God's Word.

A final external evidence that the Bible is truly God's Word is the indestructibility of the Bible. Because of its importance and its claim to be the very Word of God, the Bible has suffered more vicious attacks and attempts to destroy it than any other book in history. From early Roman Emperors like Diocletian, through communist dictators and on to modern-day atheists and agnostics, the Bible has withstood and outlasted all of its attackers and is still today the most widely published book in the world.

Throughout time, skeptics have regarded the Bible as mythological, but archeology has confirmed it as historical. Opponents have attacked its teaching as primitive and outdated, but its moral and legal concepts and teachings have had a positive influence on societies and cultures throughout the world. It continues to be attacked by pseudo-science, psychology, and political movements, yet it remains just as true and relevant today as it was when it was first written. It is a book that has transformed countless lives and cultures throughout the last 2,000 years.

6. CHRISTIANS ARE JUST A BUNCH OF HYPOCRITES.

A religious hypocrite is, by definition, a non-believer, since he is only pretending to be an adherent of the faith. A hypocrite is not a person who commits some sins on occasion (all people commit sin occasionally), but someone who practices those sins on a routine basis. The truth of the matter is that hypocrisy has been a problem for those who claim to follow God for a very long time. In fact, God challenged Cain (the first son born of Adam and Eve) on his hypocrisy when he submitted an inferior offering to Him. By far, of all preachers and prophets of the Bible, Jesus had the most to say about hypocrisy and hypocrites.

He didn't mince any words on the subject, but directly confronted the religious hypocrites of His day (the scribes and Pharisees), they hated Him intensely - eventually having Him arrested on trumped up charges.

This is the very reason we need to live out what we confess. Once we tell people we are Christians we must be ready to have our lives be under the microscope! I would also say that Christians are not perfect, we have flaws and weaknesses like all of humanity. Thanks be to God for His grace, His unmerited favor which gives us the ability to be like Christ, because it is impossible in our own strength. Paul said it this way, *1 Corinthians 15:10 (ESV) But by the grace of God I am what I am, and his grace toward me was not in vain. On the contrary, I worked harder than any of them, though it was not I, but the grace of God that is with me.*

Grace is hard to understand but I would best describe it as the ability people have to do the extraordinary. Have you ever witnessed someone being able to go through the most horrific things, and wonder how did they do that? Share with them a story of amazing grace, here's mine.

My prior pastor's wife lost her husband, mother and three sons over a two year period, all from different kinds of death. When her last son died she stood up, sick as she is herself from Lupus, and spoke of her faith in God at her son's funeral. She said that she did not blame God, and for an hour she testified about her love for her family and her Lord. I must add, this is a woman who does not like public speaking and primarily keeps to herself. I would never have imagined her having the strength to do this, but God did. That is grace at work! Her testimony spoke volumes to so many that thought she had every right to blame God, be crushed in spirit, and surely to not get up and speak of her steadfast faith in Jesus. God took what the devil meant for evil and used it to save those with ears to hear what the Spirit of God was saying.

7. IT'S NARROW MINDED TO BELIEVE THAT CHRISTIANITY IS THE ONLY WAY. THERE ARE MANY ROADS TO GOD.

Today to say your truth is the only truth is to then be pinned as narrow minded. We must distinguish that all religions are different and do not share the same truth or path to God. You may call it *narrow minded,* but the fact is if you believe the Bible is the word of God, then you have to believe all of it, and you can't pick and choose what you will believe. *John 14:6 (NASB) Jesus said, I am the way the truth and the life no man comes to the father but through me.*

The greatest difference between Christianity and all man made religions, is that none of them can forgive sins, only Jesus. All other religions require people do enough good works to offset the bad. That's an exhausting way to try and earn your salvation. It's the root of most religions.

Acts 4:12 (ESV) And there is salvation in no one else, for there is no other name under heaven given among men by which we must be saved. Josh McDowell, in his book *More Than a Carpenter,* (which I highly recommend you keep a copy on hand) wrote that there were only three options of who Jesus Christ could be: *either He is Lord, Liar, or a Lunatic.*

The truth is Jesus claimed that He was the Son of God. He was clear about His mission; He was the Lamb that would take away the sins of the world with His sacrifice. Suppose God gave people as a free gift, the promise of a future life that would be without pain, without sickness, without death, and without tears. Suppose that God said to these people, *There is one thing that I demand. I demand that you honor My only-begotten Son and that you worship and serve Him alone.* Suppose God did all of that, would you be willing to say to Him, *God, that's not fair, you are being narrow minded to ask that of me.* We can't have our cake and eat it too!

8. GOD IS TOO LOVING TO SEND ME TO HELL.

God is a God of love, but He is also a righteous judge and must judge sin. *Romans 6:23 (NIV) For the wages of sin is death, but the gift of God is eternal life in Christ Jesus our Lord.* The fact is God did not choose death for us; man did. There is no death in God, and He can only create what is in Him. *Hebrews 2:14 (NIV)* explains that since the children have flesh and blood, Jesus too shared in their humanity so that by His death He might break the power of him who holds the power of death—that is, the devil—Hell was designed for the devil and his fallen angels which we call demons.

God gave Adam and Eve free will and because they chose to eat from the tree of knowledge of good and evil, sin entered the world. God's intent was for us to live forever in communion with Him. We were not meant to die but now we will live in a dying world with an expiration date! If we have sin on us, the grave has the power to call us to hell. *Ezekiel 18:20 (NIV) The one who sins is the one who will die. The child will not share the guilt of the parent, nor will the parent share the guilt of the child. The righteousness of the righteous will be credited to them, and the wickedness of the wicked will be charged against them.*

The reason Jesus couldn't be held by death is because He was sinless and so the grave had no hold on Him. When we die if our sins are hidden in Christ, we can gain access to heaven and the Lord because the grave sees us sinless like Christ. It is His righteousness that we have available to us. *2 Cor. 5:19 explains that God was reconciling the world to Himself in Christ, not counting people's sins against them. And He has committed to us the message of reconciliation.*

I would also say to that person, "It is *because* God loves you, he sent me to tell you about His son Jesus and how He died so you could be forgiven and spend eternity in heaven. Won't you accept His free gift of salvation to escape hell and come into right standing with God?" *John 3:16-17 (NIV) "For God so loved the world, that he gave his only Son, that whoever believes in him should not perish but have eternal life. For God did not send his Son into the world to condemn the world, but in order that the world might be saved through him.* God does not send us to hell we actually send ourselves! I heard a sermon by Billy Graham where he tells a person, "So let's say there is a 50% chance you could be wrong about hell, are you willing to take that chance that you could spend eternity there?" It would be like a pilot telling you there was a 50% chance that the plane you are getting ready to board was going to crash, you would go anyway or would you heed his warning?

9. I HAVE BEEN HURT BY THE CHURCH AND DON'T NEED RELIGION.

Jesus did not die for a religion but a relationship with us. He died to free us from religious bondages. Religion has pushed many people away from church and thus away from God. We must help the person distinguish and separate their feelings about the institution of the church and Jesus Christ Himself. If we can do that, they may be more apt to accept Christ. His teachings are so loving and nothing like the disappointment and hurt they may have received from a church or particular person. Many people have been hurt by people in the church and it has tainted them. It is a shame that the very place people should feel safe has deceived and betrayed them.

I know it must grieve God to see the church act in

such a way to its own. We must be very sensitive to the past hurts and help people forgive those that have hurt them and put their trust in Jesus and not in people or the institution. The root of bitterness, if left unchecked, can fester and rob people of living in abundance. We must teach them to guard their heart by refusing to dwell on what happened, refusing to focus on the people who hurt them, and refusing to belabor the weaknesses of the church. We must also remind them that not all churches are the same and to perhaps seek out a different one. Assure them that Jesus will never leave or forsake them, based on Hebrews 13:5. He is faithful and always can be trusted. *Jeremiah 31:3 (ESV) The Lord appeared to him from far away. I have loved you with an everlasting love; therefore I have continued my faithfulness to you.*

10. YOU WORRY ABOUT YOUR LIFE AND I'LL TAKE CARE OF MINE. MIND YOUR OWN BUSINESS.

If someone is totally unreceptive, all you can do is present the truth in love. Be empathetic, and always respond with kindness. Being mean to a mean person only escalates the situation; we are called to be peaceful and "turn the other cheek." *Romans 12:18 (NIV) If possible, so far as it depends on you, live peaceably with all.* Tell them with a tear in your voice that you are not asking them to join a church or make a commitment right then but that you are genuinely concerned about people going to hell and not understanding the gospel message of eternal life. *1 Cor. 6:9-10 (ESV) Do you not know that the unrighteous will not inherit the kingdom of God? Do not be deceived: neither the sexually immoral, nor idolaters, nor adulterers, nor men who practice homosexuality, nor thieves, nor the greedy, nor drunkards, nor revilers, nor swindlers will inherit the kingdom of God.*

Tell them how much Jesus loves them and ask questions to see why they have hardened their heart. Encourage the person to consider the things you have shared. Suggest they ask God if He will not prove to them that He is real, then ask permission to pray for them. Give them a bible to read if they will accept it. Don't be surprised if they are a little hostile and defensive, the Bible tells us in *Romans 8:7 (ESV) for the mind that is set on the flesh is hostile to God, for it does not submit to God's law; indeed, it cannot.* Those that are in the flesh cannot please God.

Don't get offended if they haven't responded the way you would hope. Many people get defensive because they are feeling convicted. Don't take it personal because they are not rejecting you, but rather they are rejecting the message of Jesus Christ. It's not about you! Statistics say that someone has to hear the gospel an average of 7 times before they believe. It will happen if you continue to pray for them, love them and be an excellent example. *1 John 4:11-12 (NLT) Dear friends, since God loved us that much, we surely ought to love each other. No one has ever seen God. But if we love each other, God lives in us, and his love is brought to full expression in us.* Let them see *Christ in you the hope of glory.* Because of your excellent witness and living as you profess they will see the truth and, I believe, at some point they will desire what you have.

[13]
CONCLUSION

As I conclude this book there is so much I hope you have gleaned and will hold onto. I pray that this was not just another book, but that you will refer to it often as a guide book. That it will compel you to action and you will not bow to fear. Be bold in your declaration of what you know is true. Don't be like the man who looked in the mirror, took a good look at what he looked like, and then turned away and forgot.

James 1:21-25 (AMP) So get rid of all uncleanness and all that remains of wickedness, and with a humble spirit receive the word [of God] which is implanted [actually rooted in your heart], which is able to save your souls. But prove yourselves doers of the word [actively and continually obeying God's precepts], and not merely listeners [who hear the word but fail to internalize its meaning], deluding yourselves [by unsound reasoning contrary to the truth]. For if anyone only listens to the word without obeying it, he is like a man who looks very carefully at his natural face in a mirror; for once he has looked at himself and gone away, he immediately forgets what he looked like. But he who looks carefully into the perfect law, the law of liberty, and faithfully abides by it, not having become a [careless] listener who forgets but an active doer [who obeys], he will be blessed and favored by God in what he does [in his life of obedience].

Remember that you are an ambassador for Jesus Christ everywhere you go and never forget the authority that you walk in. You carry the Spirit of God and you are the tabernacle (movable habitation) where the presence of God can be felt and experienced. Don't underestimate the power within you to make a difference in the life of another. Through you the power of God can move and show his glory! You don't need a degree or special certification. *1 Peter 2:9 (ESV) But you are a chosen race, a royal priesthood, a consecrated nation, a [special] people for God's own possession, so that you may proclaim the excellencies [the wonderful deeds and virtues and perfections] of Him who called you out of darkness into His marvelous light.*

No matter your background you are qualified! This is your *now assignment!* You are called for such a time as this. If you choose to accept it, be prepared for a *life changing, never a dull moment, living on the edge kind of life*. For me it's the only place to be. It is where I feel the most alive and where I find fulfillment. God bless you my brother and sister in Christ, may you walk in abundance and fruitfulness as you spread the Good News!

RESOURCES

Cherie Anderson is a worship leader and ordained minister of the gospel. Her organization STW Ministries is headquartered out of Florida and seeks to save the world one soul at a time by inspiring and equipping Christians to be an effective witnesses of Jesus Christ. Her and her husband lead international mission trips, outreaches, and maintain an itinerate ministry schedule.

DISCOVER MORE AT:

🌐 **www.stwministries.org**
✉ **getfreeinjesus@gmail.com**

FOR BULK BOOK ORDERS VISIT:

🌐 **www.tallpinebooks.com**

TO BOOK CHERIE FOR A WORKSHOP OR SPEAKING EVENT CONTACT:
✉ **getfreeinjesus@gmail.com**

Music from Cherie available on Apple Music, Spotify, Amazon Music, and iTunes. Hard copies can be purchased at
www.stwministries.com

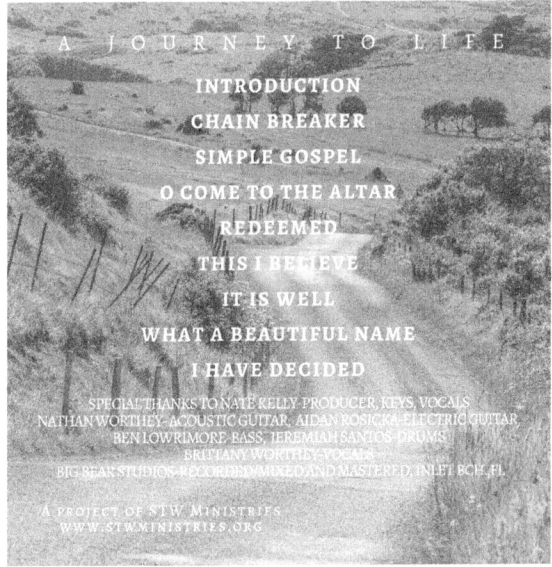

THE SIMPLE GOSPEL

CHERIE ANDERSON

A JOURNEY TO LIFE

- INTRODUCTION
- CHAIN BREAKER
- SIMPLE GOSPEL
- O COME TO THE ALTAR
- REDEEMED
- THIS I BELIEVE
- IT IS WELL
- WHAT A BEAUTIFUL NAME
- I HAVE DECIDED

SPECIAL THANKS TO NATE KELLY-PRODUCER, KEYS, VOCALS
NATHAN WORTHEY-ACOUSTIC GUITAR, AIDAN ROSICKA-ELECTRIC GUITAR
BEN LOWRIMORE-BASS, JEREMIAH SANTOS-DRUMS
BRITTANY WORTHEY-VOCALS
BIG BEAR STUDIOS-RECORDED, MIXED AND MASTERED, INLET BCH, FL

A PROJECT OF STW MINISTRIES
WWW.STWMINISTRIES.ORG

SOURCES

1. GotQuestions.org

2. Way of the Master by Ray Comfort

3. Book of Martyrs

4. Crosswalk.com: Ten Most Common Objections to Christianity

5. Complete Evangelism Book

Made in the USA
Columbia, SC
10 March 2024